Devon's Age of Elegance

Described by the Diaries of the Reverend John Swete,
Lady Paterson and Miss Mary Cornish

EDITED BY
Peter Hunt

DEVON BOOKS

First published 1984 by

DEVON BOOKS

Official Publishers to the Devon County Council

Devon Books is a division of A. Wheaton & Co. Ltd who represent a consortium of three companies:
A. Wheaton & Co. Ltd is a division of Pergamon Press

Editorial & Design
LIMELIGHT PUBLISHING LIMITED
15 Castle Street
EXETER EX4 3PT
Telephone (0392) 33186

Production & Manufacturing
A. WHEATON & COMPANY LIMITED
Hennock Road
EXETER EX2 8RP
Telephone (0392) 74121
Telex 42749 (WHEATN G)

Sales & Distribution
TOWN & COUNTRY BOOKS
24 Priory Avenue, Kingskerswell
NEWTON ABBOT TQ12 5AQ
Telephone (08047) 2690

ISBN 0 86114 750 2

British Library Cataloguing in Publication Data

Hunt, Peter
Devon's age of elegance
1. Devon - Social life and customs
2. Great Britain - Social life and
customs - 19th century.
I. Title
942.3'5081 DA670.D5

ISBN 0-86114-750-2

Photographs by Colin Johnson

This book has been produced on behalf of the Amenities & Countryside Committee of Devon County Council, by the Amenities & Countryside Officer.
Director of County Property Department, A. F. Smy

Printed in Great Britain by A. Wheaton & Co. Ltd., Exeter

Right: Ashurton, where the Rev. John Swete was born. After marrying, he bought Oxton House, Kenton, and also purchased an inn at Ashburton.

Drawn by F. Foot. Lithog[d] by W. Spreat.

ASHBURTON, DEVON.

Contents

Gateway to Oxton House.

Preface

Architecture and the style of life reached a peak of elegance during the first fifty years of the nineteenth century. It was a period when Devon's population grew and traditional ways of life changed. We still have an excellent record of these days as seen through the eyes of three diarists, foremost amongst whom was the Rev John Swete who travelled the County and recorded the rural scene, whilst Lady Paterson describes the social life of Exeter and Mary Cornish a trip taken to Plymouth to see a warship. These remarkable records are held in the Devon County Council's Archives Department in Exeter, and next door in the West Country Studies Library is a collection of prints which also illustrate the grandeur of houses and scenes at this time. Both are situated at the Central Exeter City Library.

County Councillor Roy Chapple, the chairman of Devon County Council's Amenities and Countryside Committee felt, like the rest of the members, that the public should have an easier access to these treasures and the opportunity to enjoy them in their own homes. The most appropriate way was to ask the Chief Librarian, Alison Shute, and the County Archivist, Margery Rowe, to make the material available so that this book could be compiled. Over a period of about a year this has been achieved, with considerable editorial help from the County Archivist and her staff and the West Country Studies Librarian Ian Maxted, and with the support of the former County Planning Officer John Turpin.

Not all the diaries in the possession of the County Council have been reproduced and those volumes used have had to be edited to avoid tedious philosophical discussion and to an appropriate length for those with a general rather than scholastic interest. The spelling has been modernised so that the occasional ye does not appear, 'scite' becomes 'site', etc; but place names have been left the same as they were spelt at the time, to provide a degree of authenticity and an insight to the derivation of present spellings. This has all been completed without detracting from the general sense of what was written.

Peter J. Hunt

Left: the 'Gateway to Oxton House'; from where the Rev. John Swete set out on his journeys around Devon.

1. The Age

One hundred and fifty years ago the builders of Devon created some of the finest terraces and most dignified country houses to be seen anywhere. This was the golden era of Georgian and Regency architecture, which with its scale and splendour still graces many towns today. It was a period of increasing prosperity particularly for the middle classes whose grand crescents and terraces often displayed an imposing uniformity. The stucco facades, regular windows, doors and classical columns of the more prosperous areas, were intended to report to the world that they belonged to rich, solidly respectable owners. The middle-class villas and country houses which complemented the growing number of terraces in the first half of the nineteenth century were no less imposing and recorded the taste for spacious and grand living that the successful merchant or landowner expected.

It is of course the homes of the richer people in society that are often wrongly thought to represent society as a whole. Nevertheless, throughout the country there were an increasing number of people with more spare time and broadening opportunities, and certainly even amongst those who were only moderately prosperous, there was the promise of a changing and exciting future. Oddly, some of the finest buildings which capture the confidence of the age were produced by speculative builders and surveyors using pattern books. There was no architectural profession; although the Institute of British Architects was founded in 1834 it was only after the middle of the Century that examinations were introduced to confound the artist or surveyor with a bent for building, and seems to mark the start of a general decline in house design continued with small exception until today.

A host of servants – maids, cooks, footmen, coachmen and valets – attended the wealthy and serviced their grand homes, living a considerably more rigorous and trying life than their employers. The opportunities which they had for leisure or advancement must have varied considerably, depending as much on the kindness of their master or mistress as anything else. However unsatisfactory this might seem, in some respects it would almost certainly have been a happier life than the existence of some tradesmen and labourers who crowded the ancient slums of Exeter and Plymouth. In both these towns there were parts with cramped quarters, dirty with open drains, echoing more closely the worst of medieval times than the elegant world of the nineteenth century. There were outbreaks of cholera in those overcrowded and poverty stricken slums in the early parts of the Century, and bread riots like those of 1847 in Exeter are a clear reminder of the grinding misery and hunger endured by the less fortunate from time to time during these years.

Just as not everyone lived in beautiful spacious houses, surrounded by elegant furniture, inspired by the Greek classical revival, neither were the majority confined to the filth of an urban slum. Most people lived in small towns and villages, where the number of new buildings was small. Most tried to modernise ancient property, just as is done today; but as new houses were built, even the humble ones, there was a considerable improvement in general standards. Unlike the rapidly expanding industrial Midlands where overcrowding was becoming general, Devon remained a wild and remote rural county without these problems, even in most of the larger towns. At the turn of the Century only 340,000 people lived in the County and although the numbers grew rapidly during the next fifty years to 532,000 there was a close dependance on farming and fishing and everyday life was closely bound up with these occupations. For almost everyone the edge of town was close by and life was dominated by the changing seasons and countryside pursuits and images.

The beginning and end of an age are never clearly marked, but certainly by the beginning of the Century, and coincident with the Napoleonic wars, the age of elegance was well established and fifty years later it had passed. Perhaps like most wars the Napoleonic conflict, which ended in 1815, encouraged more radical changes than would otherwise have been made. Society was throwing off the yoke of medieval thought, and the growth of leisure and the insatiable curiosity of early Victorians about every aspect of life, encouraged both the educated and the less well educated alike to delve into the mysteries of natural sciences, archaeology, history and anthropology. It was an age of romanticism based on the study of the classical past.

Devon presents a good reflection of the national trends and social changes, and it is not surprising to find that not only Plymouth and Exeter had a wide variety of learned institutes but also smaller towns, hardly larger than fair sized villages of today, also had them. Modbury's Literary and Scientific Institution with its classical facade was founded by Richard King in 1840 and in Sidmouth the London

Hotel supplied a Subscription Reading Room and there were two large libraries in Fore Street.

Many new chapels and churches were built in a religious revival that was as vigorous as the growth in literary and scientific pursuits, and throughout the County one may find Wesleyan and Baptist chapels built in the classical style. Some like those at Ashburton and Dartmouth were particularly imposing, others in smaller villages like Braunton or Chittlehampton were modest. The Anglican Church also benefited with the tremendous investment in repair and renovation of their buildings, not to mention the innumerable parsonage houses that seem to have been built.

There was a similar effort being made to provide schools, and hospitals and almshouses for the poor and elderly. National schools with free places, schools attached to churches and dame schools provided a basic education, whilst hospitals and almshouses often depended on charity. There were of course workhouses provided by society for the inpoverished as well as local and county prisons. Throughout the Century there was a remarkable growth and rebuilding. The emphasis on self-help was particularly strong and provident societies and insurance were the other side of the coin to the equally widespread charity.

Perhaps most noteworthy of all the thrusting initiatives of the age were the development of the Turnpike Trusts. In 1800 the roads of the County were still poor and the Turnpike Trusts, formed about 1753, had yet to make great improvements. Most were still only fit for the packhorse traffic that had gradually eroded rough tracks over the years into the characteristic sunken ways still forming our minor road network. The horse-drawn carriages managed on the main roads, but not easily elsewhere. By 1836 there were twenty-nine Turnpike Trusts and considerable improvements had been made, so that the main roads from the major towns were well developed, although there were plenty of minor and poorer roads which were scarcely passable at the wettest times of the year. These improved roads, and the stage coaches that travelled them, provided relatively slow access throughout the County. The coming of the railway, in 1844, signalled the beginning of swift and easy travel. In that year this Victorian triumph was welcomed to Exeter with great celebrations and by 1848 it had reached Plymouth, effectively connecting Devon to Bristol and the national network.

The river estuaries provided excellent ports for coastal trade, but the typically rolling countryside prevented the wide development of canals that had been all the rage elsewhere in the country from around the 1760s. There was of course the Exeter Canal which had been built between 1564 and 1566, the oldest in the country, and this was improved in 1827. It had served to help the city prosper as a manufacturing centre and port until after the Napoleonic wars. Another, the Grand Western Canal linked Tiverton with Taunton from about 1815, and was intended to form part of a national network, although it was mainly used for transporting goods locally.

The Stover Canal was built in 1794, financed by James Templer and went from Bovey Tracey to the River Teign near Newton Abbot with a later branch to Chudleigh which was supported by Lord Clifford and completed in 1843. The Tavistock canal ran four miles to Morwellham Quay and was intended to transport metal ores from the various copper, tin and lead mines of the neighbourhood. At this time Dartmoor was extensively mined for a variety of metals, and copper in particular was important.

In 1823/4 a small canal was cut by Lord Rolle between Great Torrington and the River Torridge below Wear Gifford where it was navigable, and the Bude Canal was also developed and extended into Devon.

The impetus for change in the nineteenth century undoubtedly came from the impact of the Napoleonic wars. Fortifications, barracks and other military provisions were made in the County but most affected of all was Plymouth. Following the threat of invasion by the French in 1798, 1803 and 1805, considerable work was put in hand to defend Plymouth town and docks. In 1811 the Great Breakwater was conceived to give a sheltered harbour for the fleet, but it took forty years to complete. The Royal Naval Hospital at Stonehouse, built in 1763, received 48,000 wounded during the war, and a new dock was opened in Devonport in 1789. After the war the value of the Navy was not forgotten and the Royal William Victualling Yard, which in its day was a magnificant national establishment, was started in 1826 and completed in 1835.

Perhaps the most lasting and spectacular monument to the war is Dartmoor Prison. In 1808/9 five enormous rectangular prison blocks were built, and these held 1,500 prisoners, taken from the overcrowded prison hulks of Plymouth. Here the French and American prisoners remained in the misty bleakness of the moor until 1815.

The record of population growth vividly illustrates the mushrooming popularity of resorts like Exmouth, Sidmouth and Torquay as well as the escalating growth of Plymouth, Exeter, Barnstaple and most of the market towns in the County. Changing almost as much were the villages and countryside. To satisfy the demands of the Napoleonic war more timber was required and more food. The quest for better ways of growing both gathered impetus, and the use of such wastes as Dartmoor were seriously considered. In 1794 Robert Frazer writing on the state of agriculture in Devon, observed that the farms were generally small, from twenty to forty acres, as a general rule, and there were relatively few of two or three hundred acres. The period of tenure, particularly in Devon and the West Country rather than elsewhere, was for ninety-nine years (seventy-nine years in Dartmouth was usual), determinable on lives. Farmers could of course occupy two, three or more holdings to increase their acreage.

Between 1800 and the middle of the Century there was a growth in the size of farms and by then the great majority of farms ran from fifty to sixty acres up to 200 or 250 acres, and leases were being made more frequently for a definite period of years rather than lives. It had been realized that the fertility of the soil could be increased by the application of lime, and after 1800 there were continuous innovations of machinery and still further enclosures of land. By the middle of the Century two-horse ploughs were universal, and light carts and waggons used. Oxen were still occasionally used and could plough an acre a day, and probably a long day at that. Today it is possible with modern machinery to plough an acre more deeply in little more than an hour, and the average wheat yield is as much as seven times more, although arguably less nutritious.

After the upheaval of the Napoleonic wars, changes from an agrarian economy to one more dependent on manufacturing, and from the social limitations imposed by an outmoded hierarchy to one more fitted to the times, lead inevitably to great reforms. The Parliamentary Reform Act of 1832 was the first of a series of important regulating acts introduced over the next twenty years. To most people the closer regulation of some aspects of their lives would have been accepted in the same way that they are today, and just as now, it was the daily meetings at markets or workplace and the gossip of the town that were most significant. Nevertheless, the importance of various changes were often widely recognised, so that remote Winkleigh commemorated the 1832 Act by erecting a pyramidal water conduit with the names of Grey, Brougham, Russell and Althorp, carved in its stone. These were the national heroes of radicals wanting reform, and worthy of recognition even at the parish pump, but there seems to have been no similar memorial to the introduction of income tax by Peel a little later, although that might be because it was taken as a temporary expediency only.

Undoubtedly the Reverend John Swete travelled the byways of Devon quite conscious of the momentous events taking place, aware of the changes, but recording the slow movement of the countryside and its ways which seemed scarcely to be threatened by war and innovation.

He was born in 1752 in Ashburton, the son of a surgeon, Nicholas Tripe. He changed his name as a condition for the inheritance of a fortune from Mrs. Swete, his godfather's widow. His fortune enabled him to live a comfortable life at Oxton House, which he rebuilt in 1781 on the site of an earlier property. For centuries the house at Kenton near Exeter had been in the Martyn family, and his mother had been a Martyn. It had come into his father's possession from William Martyn who died in 1767, but Nicholas Tripe continued his medical practice in Ashburton where he died in 1790, allowing the property to be enjoyed by his son.

John's upbringing had not been exceptional for the "squarson" class that enjoyed the leisure and opportunities of the country vicarage. He went to Eton in 1769 and on to Oxford where he graduated in 1774. He took Holy Orders in 1781 and was made a prebendary of Exeter in that year. It was evidently a busy year for him, remembering the building programme on which he had also embarked. With the example before him of Capability Brown, whom he probably met whilst the grounds of the neighbouring estate of Mamhead were being remodelled in 1779, he started to remodel the grounds of Oxton with commendable vigour. He removed the garden walls and clipped yews and replaced them so that the garden echoed the natural beauty of the valley. He records that ten years passed in this enterprise of rebuilding and laying out grounds, and it was achieved at a cost of over £6,000. This was at a time when £30 a year was an acceptable living wage. He reflects that it was fruitfully expended, and without doubt like many other landowners of his day he left an inheritance of great beauty which only now, in full maturity, is the present generation enjoying, and destroying, without replacing in an entirely satisfactory way.

In 1784 he married Charlotte Beaumont who seems to have been as prolific in her way as her husband; she produced fourteen children, four of whom died as infants. He was a gentleman of his age, accepting his good fortune without any apparent concern, a little pompous and above all having curiosity of a rather romantic kind. When he died in November 1821 at the age of sixty-nine, the age of elegance was reaching its climax. He embodied those qualities which the educated and privileged strived for, a breadth of interest and depth of observation and an appreciation of elegance.

There could scarely be a better eye witness account of Devon in

Drawn by R. Brown, Archt.

Engraved by Thos. H. Shepherd.

OXTON HOUSE, DEVONSHIRE.

THE SEAT OF JOHN BEAUMONT SWETE, ESQUIRE.

TO WHOM THIS PLATE IS MOST RESPECTFULLY INSCRIBED.

BY THE PROPRIETORS.

the age of elegance than John Swete. He had the advantages of time and opportunity to record all that might be expected to interest an educated man of the age. His descriptions in the journals and many of his amateurish watercolours (not interesting enough to reproduce in this book) convey the lost world of over a century and a half ago, and these are further supplemented by the publication of a large number of engravings by several publishers from the late 18th Century which reached a flood by the 1830s. Like Swete they recorded picturesque views of the County and the grand country houses of the famous.

No detailed descriptions of Exeter and Plymouth are available from John Swete, but Lady Paterson's diary, written at Heavitree, gives a description of the life lived by the comparatively wealthy in Exeter, whilst an extract from the diary of Miss Mary Cornish of a privileged day visiting a warship in Plymouth Sound seemed an equally appropriate inclusion. All the diarists portray different aspects of the county's life during the period from around 1800 to 1850 from the viewpoint of those with social status. Each chapter has additional information extracted from *White's Directory of Devon* for 1850, Risdon's *Survey of Devon* produced in 1810 and in the case of Plymouth from *The Tourist's Companion* being a Guide printed in 1823.

The overpowering feeling that one has when considering both journals of the time, and the prints, is of a countryside, remote as any foreign land, with secret combes and vales where at last the often eccentric and insular lives of those who lived in them were being prised open and caught up in the intrusive changes of progress. One of the greatest attractions of the time was the landslip that took place in 1839 between Lyme Regis and Axmouth, which with maturity presents an even more impelling attraction today.

The South Devon Railway and the new steamships were engraved and reproduced to mark the wonders of engineering. The growth of the resorts like Ilfracombe and Torquay are recorded with equal enthusiasm, whilst prints showing notable public buildings confirm great civic pride. The new and useful, like the Haytor Granite Quarries find their place with the wonders of nature, and are generally second to them as popular objects, although churches must rank in importance as a subject more popular than any.

William Spreat was probably the most prolific of the artists around the 1840s, and earlier the local scene was dominated by George Rowe. James Harding (1798-1863), Capt. G. R. Sartorious and Louis Haghe (1806-1885) each produced a series of excellent drawings but J. M. Turner (1775-1851) manages to portray some dramatic or interesting aspect less frequently captured by others.

2. Tour to the North of Devon

by the Reverend John Swete

Having long projected an excursion to the North of the County, on Friday the 4th of September 1789, I mounted my horse in company with two neighbouring gentlemen – the principal object of the day being to dine with a friend at Moreton.

Quitting the grounds of Oxton, we rode up Holloway lane, and having mastered a stony and steep ascent of a mile, emerging from a deep defile, we gained the level and commanding heights of Halldown – turning quick to the right we inspected a large "Barrow" known by the Country around, by the name of "Great Stoneheap", which though originally it was of a conical form, as are all the tumuli in these parts, yet being now intersected, by an opening made in the year 1780 afforded a very singular, and conspicuous object to the subjacent Country.

The prospect from hence, for its beauty and extent will not often perhaps be found rivalled. Mamheads pine clad hill! The castellated grandeur of Powderham, the more immediate rural scenes of Bickham, Trehill and Oxton – the expanse of ocean stretching to the East – the Cathedral towers rising in the North, between which through a fertile wooded vale, decorated with towns and villas of every description, are seen flowing on the widening waters of the River Exe. These form the outlines of a fine picture, the variety and splendor of which can never fail of exciting unusual admiration, passing on the ridge of the Down, after the space of a mile, we arrived at a line of elevated ground. This appears to be a continuance of the Roman road which is very discernible from the seven to the eight mile stone and which led from Exeter through Kenford to Totness.

We now traversed the northern range of the Race ground and soon after arrived in view of Halldon House, the fine seat of Sir Robert Palk.

Drawn by G. B. Campion. Engraved by Henry Wallis.

HALDON HOUSE, DEVONSHIRE.

THE SEAT OF SIR LAWRENCE PALK BART TO WHOM THIS PLATE IS RESPECTFULLY INSCRIBED BY THE PROPRIETORS.

This magnificent structure was erected by Sir George Chudleigh about seventy years ago. It hath been in the possession of Sir Robert Palk upwards of twenty years and perhaps in that space of time, scarcely any spot hath undergone such striking alterations – the hand of Taste hath directed every improvement – 'twas that which removed the walks, the fountains, and the gardens which surrounded the House, and converted then into lawns! 'twas that which made the formal Vista give place to the more pleasing and less artificial clump – and twas that, which cloathed the wild and barren hills with the Pine and the beech, and introduced the golden sheaf.

Descending Halldown to the north is a triangular tower raised by Sir Robert Palk and devoted to the memory of his friend General Lawrence. It has a round tower at each angle and rose three stories high. From its own elevation and that of the conical hill on which it was placed it became an object to the most distant parts of the County, standing on Penhill.

Bidding adieu to these fine grounds, which though they are now covered with the most thriving plantations, promising as those at Mamhead, at no very distant day to become the ornament of the Country, I yet remember to have traversed when they were, as wild and bare, as any of the other parts of Halldown. We turned down the hill towards the West and after a mile or two reached the Village of Ashton, where are the Ruins of a Mansion House belonging to the Chudleighs and the last of which Family, Sir George quitted it, having taken a predilection for the Eastern side of the hill where he erected the house I have just described, now possessed by Sir Robt Palk.

We soon after crossed the River Teign by a bridge.

Reaching a charming spot of half mile beyond Canon Teign house, to the back of which returning we mounted a steep ascent of near a mile, and passed over several small downs, on the last of which before we entered the Moreton turnpike road was seen that huge rock of granite called Blackstone.

Ere we rose from the vale to the town of Moretonhampstead, a little removed from the road we beheld an excellent Parsonage house, lowly seated at the base of the hill on which the Church forms a conspicuous object. Here making good cheer with our hospitable Friend Mr. Fynes, we passed the remainder of the day, and on the following morning, made an early excursion to the curiosities of the neighbourhood.

Reaching Whiddon house, an old edifice, of no importance finely placed though lost to all the beauties that surround it for, by stables, walls and barns it is effectively blocked up towards the Park, which is of the wildest and most romantic nature.

The scenery is uncommonly wild and singular. The Teign's source is about 10 miles distant, in the forest of Dartmoor near the Gidleigh hills, is from thence descride rolling through a narrow passage among the mountains, and after it is lost to the eye, its course is in the most desided manner pointed out by means of these mountains, which as it were thrust themselves in, one between another and over spreading in their lower parts by woods, midway abrupt and broken by crags and on the summit, smooth and covered by turf, exhibit such a variety of the sublime and the beautiful of Nature as cannot fail of rivetting the attention.

We now remounted, and after a return of half a mile, we left Drewesteignton towards the East, and rejoined the public road we had quitted near the bridge – a ride of about two miles brought us in sight of the famous Cromlech, which is one of the most perfect in the world – it stands in a field belonging to a farm called, perhaps from this curious monument, Shel-stone. I had not the least difficulty in passing under the covering stone, erect and with my hat on.

Nothing can well exceed the scenery of this place! Rocks the most grotseque and dissimilar imaginable! Vast hollows deepening into gloomy recesses in proportion to the size of the Karn, piled at one time irregularly on each other – at other mocking the nicest junction of experienced art; over which the dark green ivy trailed its parasitical branches – and from every interstice, started the Mountain Ash, beautifully decorating the scene with its orange tinted berries – from the summit of these rocks, is seen towards the South West the grounds of Rushford which (beheld at this distance) nothing could well be more romantic – the Mansion house, long deserted, lay in ruins! At Rushford, though scarcely one stone of the decayed edifice lay artifically over another yet its grounds, were delightfully spread over with waving woods and beautiful trees, single and in clumps in the midst of which rose a rocky eminence of a conical shape around whose base roared on the waters of the mantling Teign.

The little eminence, chosen for our repast, overhung what a year or two since was called Bradford pool, a vast hollow, excavated, during a succession of ages by Miners – by some enterprizing persons it had lately been drained by means of adits, drove under the hill on which the Cromlech stands. Here with regret, taking leave of my companions, who returned to their respective homes, I proceeded on my tour.

Passing over a tolerably cultivated country, contrasted on the South west by the bleak aspect of Cawson hill, I rode through the little town of South Zeal to be noticed only in that it possesses a piece of

THE ABOVE ENGRAVING WAS TAKEN FROM A DRAWING BY SWETE

Antiquity, resembling a Town-hall in the centre of the street, which from its tower at the western end, composed of four pillars enclosing a bell, would give one room to suppose at least, that in days of yore it had seen better cheer, and houses around it, not quite so mean as the present ones. Here I crossed a rivulet which hurries on to join the Taw. Leaving the town of South Tawton, famous for is limekilns which are seen encompassing it as so many bulwarks, about half mile on the right the hamlet of Stickle path next lay in my way possessing an old Chapel in a field washed by the River Taw here, a mountain stream, rapid, and of no great consequence. Not long after I reached Okehampton, a borough town not very respectable in its buildings and chiefly remarkable for its Castle, which about half a mile to the S.W. is seated on a proud eminence, beneath which runs the West Oke from whence the town derives its name.

The ruins of a magnificent castellated Pile, crowned by a Keep, high towering over the other buildings, in feudal times rendered almost impregnable by Nature and effectually made so, by an effort of Industry and indefatigable perserverance, forming a Gulph or chasm interjacent of considerable width and fearfull depth, while on every other quarter, the hill slopes away from the exterior walls, so steep and rapid.

The Park, separated by the West Oke from the Castle, is of great extent, being 9 miles in circumference, bounded on the east by the Eastern Oke, on the north and part of the west, by the Western Oke, and towards Dartmoor by a strong wall. It rises gently in most parts from the Rivers, and is highly beautified by thick woods, of almost every kind of trees, that this country can call indigenous.

Sleeping here, the next morning (being Sunday) I walked to the Parish Church, most inconveniently situated for the People of the town, being placed on the summit of a hill to the westward and at least half a mile distant.

In the Evening we mounted our horses and we had but barely proceeded a quarter of a mile behind the house, when all at once opened to the Eye such a scene as no description of mine can give any but the faintest idea of the beauty, the grandeur of the prospect exceeding every thing I had before seen of the kind – an intermixture of woods, of water, of hills rarely to be paralleled!

Great Haldon has now been substantially aforested with fir trees, but Oxton, Bickham and Trehill survive, each within mature parkland. The views from Telegraph Hill are splendid although past vantage points are often hidden in the forest, so too are some of the ancient burrows.

The triangular tower raised by Sir Robert Palk to the memory of his friend, General Lawrence in 1788 is now open to the public. Inside the tower is a statue of the General and several tablets. The view from it covers much of the County, and in turn it is a landmark for miles around.

Ashton has changed little over the years and rather like its neighbour Doddiscombsleigh is a scattered village with some good cob and thatch buildings which have been there for centuries. Canonteign House is to the west of the Teign which the diarist probably crossed at Spara Bridge, set close to some fine broadleaved woodlands.

The direct path to Moretonhampstead which is the gateway to the high moorland would have passed over what is now coniferous plantations surrounding Tottisford and Kenwick reservoirs. At Shilstone in the parish of Drewsteignton the cromlech stands six feet high.

Cawsand Beacon rises to 1750 feet to the south of South Zeal. It is bleak and has more than its fair share of stone rows, hut circles and other prehistoric remains. South Zeal lies below the A30 Exeter - Okehampton Road and interestingly keeps its medieval burgage plots which have existed from the time it was built as a new town. The hedge boundaries that mark these relatively narrow strips are clearly seen unaffected by the sporadic modern development. The old granite cross and ancient chapel with two bells and four pillars, which was used in 1850 as a school, stands in the road close to the Oxenham Arms, which is an attractive fifteenth century granite building. At the higher end of the street is the Kings Arms which itself is probably sixteenth century and might well be thought a worthy rival.

South Tawton is a neat village with the church of St. Andrew standing in the centre of a cluster of ancient and pleasant houses with a granite church house amongst them. Sticklepath is a larger village which time has not passed by in the same way as it has South Tawton. The A30 passes through it bringing rather too much noise and traffic. In Victorian days it was a thriving little town with two chapels two inns and corn, bone, and woollen mills. The mills have gone, although when entering Sticklepath from Exeter it is possible to see a waterwheel slowly turning, and used to generate electricity for a private house, whilst half way through the village with its thatched and stone buildings, opposite the Taw River Inn, is The Finch Foundry, a working museum, where waterpower drives the hammers to bend iron into horse shoes or traditional farm implements. A display of traditional implements complement the mill itself, and for the thirsty it's possible to enjoy a good cup of tea there.

THE FINCH FOUNDRY, STICKLEPATH

Okehampton is only a short way from Sticklepath and has grown into a large market town. In effect the A30 main road widens into what, if it were not hidden by passing and parked cars, is a long square with the ancient St. James Chapel closing it at the east end, whilst at the western end it narrows and curves up hill. The All Saints parish church was rebuilt shortly after fire destroyed the original one in 1842. A market is still held in the town and the modern market hall is part of a neat new shopping area. The Independent Chapel was built in 1822 and the Wesleyan one in 1841, and the National and Infant Schools around the same time. These served the whole parish which had grown from 1400 in 1801 to 2,200 in 1850. Even with a relatively small population it was well serviced, with most trades listed. There were eleven mills and three eating houses and like most small thriving towns there was considerable opportunity to learn a trade and follow it. Rather unexpectedly there appear amongst them straw hat makers, a comment on the styles of the 1850s, and perhaps less surprisingly three surgeons (doctors) and seven stone masons. The latter might maliciously be thought to have been trying to keep up with the mistakes of the town's medical profession!

The ruins of Okehampton Castle are a romantic sight set close to wooded parkland to the west of the town. It was an eleventh century building which had a Mott and Bailey, and modernised in the fourteenth century to become a family home of the Courtenays who laid out the Deer Park. The extensive area occupied by the Castle, before it was pulled down in 1534, indicates its earlier strength and grandeur.

Drawn by J. M. W. Turner, R. A.

Engraved by J. Willmore.

Okehampton.

Devonshire.

After breakfast I left the hospitality of Kerslake and crossing the turnpike road in front of the house, I journeyed over extensive commons for several miles having a distant catch towards the N.W. of Ashbury the seat of Woolcombe Esq. – then entered the road leading to Hatherleigh. The Country tame, and of no attraction.

Hatherleigh is a very mean town, on a red soil, the church decorated with a spire, and seated on a ridge of elevated ground somewhat further on towards the West, about half a mile from the road, I saw Inwardleigh Church the tower of which was in a most ruinous state, having been reduced to two thirds of its height, about a year or so since by lightning.

Not long after I reached Heanton, a seat of Lord Orford, a vast pile, built at different periods – having a date of 1639 engraved in a tablet of moorstone, which is certainly from the architecture, not the oldest, but simply ascertaining the time in which the Portal, over which it is placed, was erected – from the figure of the House, which wears the form of the letter E in its front the period of its erection may possibly be determined.

The principal rooms of the house are a large hall, a dining room, in either wing, and a vast number of bed chambers furnished with antique beds decorated with network, flowers and other embroidery – one bed was in a recess, and another, probably the one, of state, was separated from the other part of the room by a railing breast high, with a door at each end giving the whole an appearance, not only of snugness but of grandeur. It has been hung with silk, and ornamented with Paintings, but the one was faded and rent and the others, that were not daubings, had long been removed to form part of the Houghton Collection. In a small room, over the doorway was a trap covering in the floor, which by a step ladder led to a lower room about eight feet square, where Colonel Rolle secreted himself, apprehensive of the then Minister Sir Robt Walpole, whom, in a fit of passion he had struck.

Having been here hospitably entertained by Mr. Mallet the Steward the next morning I proceeded on through a pleasant track of country towards Torrington. Having past a villa by the road side, belonging to Mrs. Cleveland commanding an extensive range of country, and arriving within a mile of the Town, I turned in, through a lawn to Cross, the charmingly situated seat of H. Stevens Esq. – placed on an eminence the grounds declining rapidly from the front it of course comprehends all the subjacent country, and the opposite hill on which the town of Torrington, full in view, exhibits a conspicuous and romantic object. The Houses on the South verging towards a precipice, and suspended as it were over the river Towridge, meandering round the bottom in a wavy channel with its waters kissing the very margin of the meadows "without oveflowing, full!"

Accompanied by Mr. Stevens I went in quest of the Priory of Frithelstoke, in the way which we descended to the bridge at the S.W. end of Torrington, which passing over, we again rose up a steep hill, introducing us to a common, precipitous towards the River but having a delightful prospect on the North of 'Beam', a seat of Dennis Rolle Esq, a most lovely and sequestered spot, protected on every side by the richest woods of the finest amphi-theatrical form, the roots of which were washed by the river, which, as if enamoured of the spot winds round it in many a meander and seems reluctant to retire from it. On the summit of an hill, three miles from Cross, having again passed the Towridge by another bridge, we came to the Ruins of the Priory which though not grand nor extensive have a good deal of the Picturesque in them and possess a pecularity in the rounding of the Western windows of the Chapel, rarely, if at all to be met with.

In our return we made a circuit through the Town of Torrington, the northern street through which we entered, though not elegant, was yet neat and ornamented with several very decent looking houses. This brought us to the centre of the Town, by the Church side, the tower of which is rendered a conspicuous object at a distance possessing an handsome spire cased with lead. In this part was also a reputable town-hall opening into a small square or Market Place – hence we passed on to the Eastern Cliffs, on the verge of which once stood a Castle. An area of an acre and a half adjacent hath been used as a bowling green, till (being in the possession of Mr. Rolle) it was suppressed by him a year or two since on account of the reputed dissipation of the gentlemen of the town, who were accustomed (it seems) now and then to game, and if fortune proved adverse, to execrate that fortune by words which were deemed not proper for Gentlemen of Character and decorum to make use of. The consequence is that its turf is destroyed – its fences broken down, and a pleasure house dismantled, which (suspended over a prodigious precipice) took in at one view a most extensive prospect, towards the South, the West and East the river serpentizing round its base, and losing itself at some distance in the fine woods which belong to Mr. Stevens, whose seat is also one of its most ornamental objects.

T. Allom T. Dixon

ROLLE CANAL, & ROLLE AQUEDUCT, NEAR TORRINGTON, DEVONSHIRE.

PETER JACKSON, LONDON & PARIS

Hatherleigh is in one of the bleaker parts of Devon although situated pleasantly enough north of the River Lew which flows northward to the Torridge. During the first half of the Century about 1800 people lived there mainly getting a living by rural pursuits. A new Market House was built in 1840 in the centre of the town but in 1970 it was removed to allow a small attractive square to be created, with several shops and the old National School, built of an attractive stone in 1838, overlooking it. After a fire sometime before 1840 the principal street which curves up from the low lying land by the River Lew, was widened and a number of houses rebuilt. There are nevertheless several ancient buildings with great stone chimneys beside it. A cattle market is still held in the town, as they have always been. The church with its spire is built of red sandstone and was enlarged and modernised about 1834, leaving some of the more ancient fittings alone. At the same time a vicarage was built for the incumbent.

Heanton Satchville in its spacious parkland was burnt down in about 1810 and an elegant Regency Mansion replaced it until again around 1950 the property was burnt down and then rebuilt. The countryside of central Devon has poorer soils, the culm measures with cold clays do not produce the most prosperous or obviously attractive landscapes, although modern drainage has changed their appearance and made them more productive.

Torrington is a remarkably unspoilt town in splendid countryside, built on a high ridge with a precipitous hillside down to the Torridge below. The town hall which was built in 1861, stands in the central square which has a cosy human scale. The red brick and stone town hall's importance is more pronounced by the central projection, being carried over the pavement on rounded arches. Amongst the eighteenth century buildings in the square the older attractive Black Horse Hotel adjacent to South Street has a plaster panel above a fireplace inscribed "TD SD 1681", and probably dates from then. The pannier market building is on South Street with its weather vane telling its age, 1842, as well as the direction of the wind.

The castle has entirely disappeared but the bowling green, which was in business in 1850, is still used, one hopes without too many harsh words. The pleasure house mentioned by Swete may well be the octagonal gazebo, and the walls along the rear of properties here could be built with re-used stone from the castle. Not far away is the Waterloo Monument, an obelisk standing on the common land at Castle Hill below the town, which was presented by the ladies of Torrington in 1816.

The town changed considerably in the fifty years after Swete's visit. The National School was built around 1835 and a new spire was provided for Torrington Church. There were four indepedant chapels and Lord Rolle cut a short canal from the town to Wear Gifford in 1823-4. The pleasant stone toll house by the sixteenth century Taddiport bridge over which Strete passed was erected in 1830. At this time the production of woollens in the town suffered a recession so that only glove makers thrived here in 1850. Instead of these trades, today there is a small industrial estate with a factory making Dartington glass and, by Taddiport Bridge, is Torrington Creamery. There is a cattle market held in the town just as it was 150 years ago.

The normal accretions of modern buildings and an increase in its population - from around 3,300 in 1850 to 4,100 now have created inevitable changes, but it remains a delightful town and still keeps two magnificent buildings worthy of note, Palmer House visited by Dr. Johnson and Sir Joshua Reynolds and 28 South Street which was built in 1701 with some excellent plasterwork. The marvellously situated Beam House grandly standing by the Torridge as it meanders around it, and once owned by the Rolles is now Beam College. The remains of Frithelstock Priory stand unchanged next to the parish church of St. Mary and St. Gregory.

TORRINGTON

T. Allom. M. J. Starling.

FRITHELSTOKE PRIORY, DEVONSHIRE.

PETER JACKSON, LONDON & PARIS.

Left Cross on Wednesday Morn through Torrington towards Bideford. The country pleasant, the bottoms and steep aclivities of many hills warmly wooded and varied with Gentlemens Villas, amongst which was Stephenstone, another principal seat of Mr. Rolle – about 3 mile east.

The village of Tawstock, on a charming conical knoll overspread with cattle, who in the miday heat, were on this eminence, sniffing in the refrigerating breezes from the sea, and beyond the broad back of what I might almost call a mountain, beautifully empurpled with heather.

Entering through a gateway of ancient date, by the stables, I arrived in front of Tawstock House, the seat of Sir Bourchier Wrey, which when completed (for it is now but a shell) will be one of the finest houses in the County. Seated on an eminence, the grounds gently expanding on each side covered with wood – beneath – the River Taw flowing through wide spreading meadows – Tawton on the skirts of them and hills rising pleasingly above. The Church of Tawstock however at the bottom of the lawn intercepts the middle of the view, and though in a great measure concealed by plantations, yet cannot but be considered, as an object that one would have wished in a less conspicuous situation. Within however it claims particular attention not only from its form and spaciousness but from the many highly-wrought Family Monuments.

Towards Bideford – the prospect also improved and at once opened upon a noble expanse of water, over which a bridge consisting of 24 arches and of the length of 670 feet conducted one to its North side, where I found an Inn, not proportionate to the appearance of the town though possessed by civil people and affording a very good breakfast.

The town itself is very neat. Cleveland owned by Mr. Tapley, beyond and higher yet appeared the old family Mansion of the Sibthorpes, and on the banks of the river beneath, trended the little watering village of Instow. The sands which formed the fine bason of Barnstaple the seat of Col Basset and the high grounds beyond terminated this part of the view – but nearer the eye on the left a Cliff presented itself behind which lay the town of Appledore.

Barnstaple doth not as many other old towns discover its antiquity by its buildings, for these in general seem of modern date and possess a neat and handsome appearance – there are several good streets, and in them a church, and several meeting houses of Dissenters from the Church Establishment. The Quays trend on by the River, and on the North side of the principal one, rises a Portico, or Colonnade of 14 Pillars, where the Mayor and corporation were once accustomed to transact business – but where they now met (as a person walking in it informed me) not infrequently to pour out libations to the God Bacchus – which eventually led them to excess and put the incorporated Topers to public shame.

Close by was a Religious House founded by Judhael de Totonais and consecrated to the Virgin Mary, or rather to Mary Magdalen. In the garden of this Priory was found the figure of a Knight lying Cross-legged with his sword and shield – the Remains of this house are but few.

More to the North is a vast Mount, the Keep of a Castle, here built by Athelstan (as some say) but according to others, by the above Judhael. From hence there is a noble Prospect, including most of the Points I have before noticed.

On the banks of the Taw I found an exceeding pleasant terrace walk, of very considerable length, and kept gravelled in most excellent order, which however seemed to fail in attraction for the Ladies of the Town, who, during the whole evening, universally gave the preference to a promenade on the Bridge which was not only a rough pave, without any causeway but was very subject to the inconveniences, incident to every common frequented passage of cattle, carriages, dust, etc. Possibly the fair Ladies of Barnstaple may have a pecularity of taste; or possibly they may have a predilection for the Bridge, which was in part indebted to their own sex for its erection – Tradition hath handed it down that when the rest of the Bridge was raised by the munificence of one Stamford of London – three of its pillars, or Piers were built by the "Maids of the town".

The trade of this place is of late very much reduced – especially in the Woollen manufactory – for whereas it formely maintained fourscore Combers, it now possessed but four – its other Commerce consists of the conveyance of coals from Wales, and of coasting Voyages, of but little import or advantage. On its decay (which may be owing in a great degree to the Havens, being more shallow and full of sandbanks than formerly) its neighbour Bideford hath risen!

The following morning passing over another bridge, I rode through the village of Pylton, at the end of which, I observed a Pillar 10 feet high and about 6 inches in circumferance, standing on a rising ground, on the right of the road. The people of the place could give no account of its erection.

T. Allom — Tombleson.

BIDEFORD BRIDGE & TOWN, NORTH DEVON.

Bideford Bridge nowadays carries considerable traffic and provides a picturesque link with former times, since there has been a bridge here for 600 years. In 1850 there were about 5,500 people living in the town, most of them on the west bank, where the Quay is still used by small coastal vessels and fishing boats. Since then the town has more than doubled in size extending beyond the older streets up and over the hills into modern estates beyond. It is an attractive town, especially the High Street and Bridgland Street where many buildings go back to the early eighteenth century.

Instow has grown into an attractive resort, facing onto the Taw/Torridge estuary with hotels, some of them converted from large Victorian houses, providing attractive accommodation. There were no more than a hundred houses here in 1850 and fewer still fifty years before. Across the water and the holiday sands is Appledore and its shipyard - a traditional craft carried on here and in Bideford.

Barnstaple like Bideford was a port in 1850 with the river navigable for sailing vessels about three miles above the town. It had more than doubled its population to 7,900 in fifty years. The addition of Pilton and part of Bishops Tawton parish following the Reform Acts of 1832 and 1835 gave a population of 11,000. The growth of the town with elegant terraces like Trafalgar Lawn and Union Terrace was quite substantial and their was much rebuilding within the old medieval town around Boutport Street and the High Street. The ancient quays, with Queen Annes Walk built in 1708 for the benefit of merchants, were used for importing goods from the Baltic, France, Spain, Portugal and North America. The old quay is now used for buses and Queen Annes Walk for an old persons' rest room.

A threatre was built in 1834, and an Assembly room in 1800, where balls and concerts were frequently held. In 1845 the Literary Institution was established in a large house in the High Street.

In line with other places the activity of the various churches suggests dedication and enthusiastic effort, and two district churches, St. Mary Magdalen in 1846 and Holy Trinity in 1847 were built. St. Peter and St. Paul with its ancient lead spire stands in the very centre of the town of the High Street and with the nearby almshouses is a picturesque reminder of quieter times.

The prosperity of the town was based on the manufacture of woollen goods, lace, paper, leather and pottery. There was also a ship building yard, several stocking weavers, brush makers and rope makers. Pottery is still made in Barnstaple and a glove making factory that was the last relic of the extensive textile business closed some years ago. The River Yeo is now used by barges bringing sand and gravel to the town as well as by a number of pleasure boats, but no boat building is undertaken. It has always been a market town and has a lively Friday market, held in the hall built for it in 1856. A cattle market is also held in the town and may shortly be moved from its present location by the Castle Mound out of the centre. The Guildhall which is now used by the town council and social service volunteers was built in 1826 and faces onto the High Street. It is a dignified building in the Grecian style and has the Barnstaple coat of arms on the pediment.

In 1850 it was a busy place with three banks and two weekly newspapers. Carriers took goods to most parts of North Devon, and the Steam packet Water Witch, which went to Bristol, called at Penhill Docks twice a week in summer and once in the winter. Sailing vessels left the town for Bristol, Liverpool and London taking passengers and trade with them.

The old medieval street pattern and small shops are still a feature of the town and the rail link with Exeter which came in 1854 is still in business. It is a modest line more linked with calm beauty than roaring commerce. The castle mound from which Swete was able to view the town was planted with trees at the beginning of the nineteenth century when it was a favourite recreation spot for Barumites. In recent years the castle green has been relieved of its Victorian buildings and left a pleasant open space. It is simply a homely market town unspoilt by overpowering buildings or brash commerce, the adminstrative centre for North Devon.

Pilton remains a village within the town, with the Parish Church and almshouses at the top end of a steeply rising street, hemmed each side with attractive little houses and shops. There is no sign of the ancient stone pillar mentioned by Swete however.

Drawn by G.B. Campion

Engraved by I. Henshall

BARNSTAPLE QUAY,
DEVON.

London. Published by R. Jennings & W. Chaplin 62 Cheapside

From the summit of an ascent which brought me to Swannon Down about 7 miles from Barnstaple I had a most charming and extensive prospect, commanding the island of Lundy, Hartland Promontory, Bideford, Appledore, Barnstaple, and the fine reach of waters, spreading onwards to either town.

A mile or two ere I came to Ilfracombe, a scene extremely romantic, of wild mishapen rocks, towering to the skies presented itself. Soon after the Church appeared, seated on an eminence above the town, of which riding through a long descending street for near a mile, I at length reached the Quay, where the Inn was situated.

The trade of this town consists for the most part in coasting voyages from Wales, transporting coals from Pembrokeshire and Glamorgan to Cornwall and bringing back copper and tin, which are rendered a marketable commodity at the smelting houses of Neath, Swansea and other places where Coal most abounds.

Within a few years indeed, another article of Commerce hath been revived, which for the space of forty years had been unaccountably disused. I allude to the capture and seasoning of Herrings, which at periodical times are here taken in vast quantitites, and (being cured) are afterwards exported to the Continent. In addition to these articles of commerce I must not omit a manufactory for rope and cordage, which is carried on to a considerable extent, and which finds a ready sale amongst the numerous vessels which frequent this port – than which a more commodious one is not to be met with, on the Northern coast of Somerset, Devon or Cornwall, the harbour having the advantage of a lighthouse, and, of being secured by a strong and handsome pier build by the Ancestors of Sir Bouchier Wrey to whom the Manor belongs.

Returning through a part of the long street and ascending a steep hill towards the East, I had a charming farewell view of the town, the lighthouse, the harbour, and the wild mountainous rocks, which environ it, forming an uncommonly eccentric and romantic scenery.

The road, which was rugged and intricate brought me to the village of Berry or Berrynharber, of no note.

I at length reached the long scattering – dilapidated Village of Coombe – Martyn lying in a fertile vale or coombe and bearing the adjunct of its ancient Landlords the Martyns whose inheritance it was many ages past, and whose principal Mansion was at Oxton from whence I set out on this excursion – being now a possession of mine, who am maternally descended from this family – my grandmother being a Martyn of this house.

The hills in this parish were in former times much noted for Mines of Copper and tin – though more so, for the silver which it produced. The discovery of this precious metal was made in the time of Edward the first and so great was the ardor of Enterprise that no less than 337 Miners were engaged from the Peak of Derby to work in these mines. In the reign of Edward III they yielded that King great Profits towards carrying on the French wars – from that period they were neglected till the days of Queen Elizabeth to whom was presented, a cup here made, by the Earl of Bath.

Since the period of Elizabeth they have been again discontinued working, till within a year or two, when another attempt was commenced by some Gentlemen of Cornwall, who however seem not very adventurous – the miners being limited to four.

From Coombe Martyn, slow, and not devoid of apprehension from the steepness and ruggedness of the road I passed on to Parracombe, a small village, the Church of which stands unaccompanied by any building saving the Clergymans on the skirts of an extensive common, and being highly placed was surrounded by Pastures of finer verdure, and fields of Corn, of more plentifull produce than might have been expected. As the road often ran on the summits of very elevated hills, I was often gratified with views of the sea, and of the coast of Wales, tho the latter through the haziness of the Atmosphere was but dimly seen. From Parracombe I journeyed pleasantly over downs till within a mile of Linton from whence a rapid and stony descent brought me to the village.

In the early nineteenth century Ilfracombe was a port with a considerable coasting trade and had a fishing fleet which caught great quantities of herring. It was also a market town with two cattle fairs and a Saturday pannier market. From 1820 the town also became a popular holiday resort and rows of houses and handsome marine villas were built on the steep sloping hills. There were about 1800 living in the parish at the turn of the century and by 1841 it had doubled in size.

The harbour is a natural rock basin and the town was reputed to have the best bathing beaches in north Devon. There were Baths built in classic style and public reading rooms in Coronation square. It could be classified as an improving town encouraged greatly by the now defunct railway and generally better communications. As well as the Parish Church three independent chapels and a National School were built in the period of expansion.

The popularity of Ilfracombe as a holiday resort has grown and the prosperity, which it has brought is limited to a seasonal kind. It is still a remote

J. Harwood. J. Thomas.

BERRYNARBOR, NEAR ILFRACOMBE.

and beautiful place with fine views from the cliff tops and within easy reach of Exmoor, and with a ferry service to Lundy.

Berrynarbor is a pleasant village overlooking Combemartin cove and within the parish is Watermouth Castle, built in 1825, and now used as a holiday camp. Combe Martin is a long village built within the steeply sloping confines of the hills on either side of its main street as it runs towards the cove. Today it depends a great deal on the holiday trade and although its buildings are not especially attractive the surrounding hills and cliffs are very picturesque. Half way through the 19th Century it was a decayed market town with a few fishing smacks and coal vessels calling in for pilots to take them through the Bristol channel. There were unsuccessful attempts to make a profit from the silver mine here in 1800, 1813 and 1817. Later in 1837 they were reopened and worked for a number of years, but since 1875 they have been closed.

Parracombe amongst high downs close to Exmoor is remote and unspoilt, with two churches, that seen by Swete, and a later one in the village built in 1878.

Combmartin North Devon

From the borders of the church yard as I sat on a projecting rock at the close of day, my eye ran over one of the most grand, wild and picturesque scenes conceivable. Towards the East it looked down a rough deep precipice on the sea, and on the West it dwelt on the woodland recess, the rocks and waterfall. Such delicious scenery at the twighlight hour of a calm and autumnal day had the most pleasing effect on my sensations.

The next morning I sallied forth, in quest of the "Valley of Stones" (considered as the chief attraction of the place) which lies to the west of the Village, at the distance of half a mile. The Scenery at this spot was of a different kind from any I had ever met with. The hills at first sloped on towards the West, spotted with loose detached rocks, which in several parts lay scattered about the bottom. Soon the tops of the succeeding hills became more and more wild and craggy – taking the shapes of disparting towers, gigantic obelisks and a thousand other fantastic forms – on the left, barely at the entrance of the Vale rose in similar manner the craggy hills. At first indeed more smooth, and at places, not inaccessible, cultivated in patches with potatoes – traces of industry thus obtruding themselves into the barren Valley, enter not into the wildness of the scenery but violate, as it were, the solemn solitude with which the eye and the mind have begun to be entertained, and point out unpleasantly, that one hath not totally quitted the haunts of Society. The gradation of their sloping side which not unfrequently ended in an headlong precipice – the variety of their stupendous rugged forms, together with those rocky fragments, which, broken from their shivered bases, had, during a succession of ages, rolled into the narrow plain, struck me with amazement.

From hence (being through a trifling accident unable to walk) I on horseback descended gradatim and with the utmost caution a very bad Alpine way adown a mountain all but perpendicular.

Having now descended about a third part of the hill, and gaining an angle of turning where the way was wider, there I stopped – being enabled without apprehension to gaze around. The two rivulets, called the east and West Lin, now became more conspicuous – they were beneath my feet and I saw them hurrying onward over many an obstructing rock to the sea forming a conflux ere they lost themselves in the depth of waters.

The little Quay rises on the Western side of the Rivers just below their junction and possesses several very decent houses. Beneath it is a Wear, marked out in the Waters by a succession of long poles where salmon are caught and (at the particular season of Spawning) Herrings in great abundance. These pass over the wear, in immense bodies at

APPLEDORE AND INSTOW.

high water and at the ebb of a low tide, are left in the shallow stream where they are easily captured. The Salmon also enter these little rivers for the same purpose; not contented however with depositing their spawn at the mouth, they force their way towards the source, delighting to leap over the opposing rocks, which at many places in deeper and more mountainous channels they effect to an almost incredible height.

As I returned from the beach, and the charming little green which borders it, the picturesque arch of a bridge over the west Lin struck me with such admiration that I immediately dismounted, and forcing my way through brambles and briars, I soon got a perfect view of it so as to take a sketch.

Taking a guide to conduct me over the downs to Castle Hill, the seat of Lord Fortescue, on Friday Sept. 11th I quitted Linton. Ascending the steep hill I the day before had passed down, and proceeding on the same track to Parracombe, at the centre of the village I turned out of the Ilfracombe road, and by a rough ascent rising towards the South I attained the high ground of Rowleigh common, over which having rode for three miles, nearly on quitting it, I perceived on the west of the track a large Burrow which had been opened in several places, and was in diameter about 100 feet. Its situation was but a little way from the bottom of the Down I had passed, and was contiguous to the lonely farm of Carbrocken burrow, deriving its name from the adjoining tumulus.

From hence I again mounted another down called Bratton, where I had the finest riding imaginable – the turf as smooth as that of a bowling green and nearly as level – commanding an extensive view of the circumjacent country, in which circular survey might be descried, Youlston the seat of Sir John Chichester on the N. West and nearer at hand Arlington – Mr. Chichesters – the tower of Bratton, Hartland point, and towards the East, receiving its bounds from Exmoor.

On every one of these eminences I discovered Beacons, at times several together – all of them in the form of Burrows, saving that they were not conical.

Having quitted this beautifull plain I rode up a steep ascent to the top of Mockham Down, where I discovered an encampment. Its situation was such, as to have given it very considerable strength, and to have enabled the Camp to have discerned an approaching enemy at distance.

Four miles riding from hence (where I dismissed my guide) over an inclosed country and good roads brought me to Castle Hill.

The Gardener attending I rode through Lord Fortescue's grounds, passing before the front of the house of no extraordinary beauty. Very little taste had been displayed in the spreading on before it, a wide space of gravelled terrace, which is raised above the subjacent lawn and fenced from it by a balustrade, having hinted my ideas on the deformity of the Appearance I was pleased with the information that this old stile was to be abolished, and that the lawn was to ascend gradually with Nature's best embellishment to the front door.

I now skirted a fine ancient wood, decorated with many capital oaks and ascending a hill arrived at a Spa – a chalybeate water of considerable strength and colour – the middle front of this building is encrusted with old roots of trees and moss in a good stile and the cell is of similar construction, having in its centre a receptacle for the mineral water. The view from hence is of no small beauty – the Eye glances over the summits of the woods before passed through, takes in a gazebo Castle upon an edifice behind the house, and all the environs of the House itself.

Having descended a hill, winding through this wood, I reached a little gate at the bottom which opened into the meadows, and where the first object that presented itself was an artificial fall of water, like a wear, on the river Bray which occupying the whole width of the channel, at this time appeared insignificent. The ride now trended on the banks for a while when it again lost itself in a thick wood where every object but the side screens of trees and brushwood was excluded – a building of two stories now presented itself, which is intended to be fitted up for the reception of Strangers, where they may take a cold repast or drink their tea, for there is no Inn near. I soon after crossed the public road and entered the Park – here having rode over a well-constructed rustic bridge and passing by a natural fall of the whole river, about ten feet high, and very picturesque, at the end of the Park where the wood begins to be very thick, I arrived at the Hermitage, which struck me, as having been executed with taste and propriety.

Returning by a fine terrace over the rustic bridge, I quitted the grounds of Castle Hill, which, though not possessing much of the romantic, have a good deal of the pleasing and the picturesque.

On the way to South Molton I passed by a fabric of elder days the ruins of which denoted former worth, though the only part now habitable being converted to a farm house belonging to Lord Fortescue.

South Molton hath nothing apparently to attract a stranger's notice, saving a kind of Square, decently built and clean – its streets are but of mean appearance – a walk leads to the Church (through a range of trees, forming a rather pretty communication with the central part

Drawn by G.B.Campion. Engraved by J. Henshall.

CASTLE HILL, DEVONSHIRE.

THE SEAT OF THE RIGHT HONOURABLE, HUGH EARL FORTESCUE, F.S.A.& D.C.L. LORD LIEUTENANT OF THE COUNTY OF DEVON; TO WHOM THIS WORK, WITH HIS LORDSHIP'S PERMISSION IS MOST RESPECTFULLY DEDICATED

BY THE PROPRIETORS.

London: R. Jennings & W. Chaplin, 62, Cheapside, 1830.

of the Town) and the Church itself large and handsomely built, rises on an eminence, and appears an object of importance.

In August 1952 after days of continuous drizzle and rain the spate from Exmoor into the East and West Lyn was so great that the already swollen and boiling rivers became raging torrents which swept with such forces through their valleys that they eventually burst their banks, changing the normal course of the river. Twenty-eight bridges were destroyed and ninety-three houses in and close to the village of Lynmouth were demolished or damaged.

During the previous 150 years it had gradually become a small holiday resort with a very good summer trade. Sharing the traffic conjestion and benefits of this trade is Lynton which stands above it on a high hill, and connected with Lynton by a funicular railway. The continuing prosperity of Lynmouth is a measure of the success with which it was rebuilt in the same scale as its earlier buildings after the disastrous storm.

Like Ilfracombe the villages grew greatly between 1830 and 1850. Both were able to provide good lodgings for the increased numbers of holidaymakers who had discovered the pleasures of the beach and beauties of the surrounding hills and vales. The steep rocky valleys of the East and West Lyn are clothed in oak and ash, and a magnificent sight. The glories of the valley of stones, with bolder tourist promotion, is now the valley of rocks, and is impressive scenery.

The hilly countryside around the fringes of Exmoor in North Devon produces more sheep than most other places in the country. Swete's trip to Castle Hill at Filleigh was across an empty windswept countryside, with beech trees shaped lopsided by the prevailing west winds. The closer to the Fortescue's seat at Castle Filleigh one gets, the more wooded and cultivated is the countryside. This magnificent house still used by the Fortescues was first built in 1740, although the central part was burnt down in 1934 and subsequently rebuilt to match the Georgian original, and stands proudly above the Barnstaple to South Molton Road. Its fine mature parkland are an unchanging pleasure, and have the ruin of a sham castle in the woods behind the house and a triumphal arch at the end of an avenue on the hillside which it faces.

There were about 4,500 people living in South Molton in 1850, showing a growth of 2000 in fifty years. Like Tiverton a number of its principal streets had been widened and paved in these years, but over the ages the pleasant little square has changed little although a number of the buildings facing it have been rebuilt or replaced. The most important of these was the Guildhall and Market Building completed in 1810. The Guildhall, built on pillars and projecting over the pavement is now used by the Town Council for its meetings and overlooks the attractively paved square.

It had all the trades that a country town could expect and considerable social activity including the building of an Independent Chapel in 1834 and a Wesleyan Chapel in 1822, together with a National School in 1834. The Parish Church of St. Mary, approached by a neat path from the Square overspread by pollarded limes, was enlarged and modernised in 1833, with further improvements about thirty years later.

A small long-unused town gaol built around 1830 has only recently been demolished to make way for new development. In 1850 one large woollen mill employing 150 people remained of several that had until this time produced serges. The town now depends on various small industries, its market and work in Barnstaple.

LYNMOUTH

Lynmouth, on the coast of North Devon.

The road from hence to Tiverton passing by Bishops Nympton and Rackenford was very hilly, very stony, and affording a view of a very tame and meagre country, till within a few miles of Tiverton when it assumed a more verdant and fertile aspect. In the west suburbs through which I entered, I was struck with an uncommon building of a very antique form – a chapel – having a turret at one end, where a bell hung to call the little community to daily prayers – by an inscription which was engraven in stone and extended (in old characters) throughout the whole length of the front, I learnt that it was an Alms House, built and endowed by John Waldron a merchant of the town in the year 1519. On passing a bridge over the River Exe, I rode through a street ornamented by several very elegant houses and by a modern handsome built church. On the North East end of the town the old Church is seated, covered over on its southern side with arms and a variety of emblematical devices. A large venerable pile, which hath attached to it a grand Tower of considerable thickness and height. Contiguous to the Churchyard are the Remains of a Castle placed on an eminence falling precipitately on the North towards the River from whence the view is now entirely blocked up by a grove of immensely high ashes and beech. At the west end it hath a square tower – another on the South East of a rounded form, enriched with ivy which hath a fine effect when contrasted with the stone of the Building which is of a reddish cast.

This tower, rising from the bank which formed one side of the moat, now converted into a Garden, the Pile of Buildings, and the fine old trees, exhibit a pleasing and picturesque scenery. On the front where the Gateway is, and over the present entrance the battlements have been destroyed and a modern roof of slate hath usurped its place – perhaps as it hath now for ever done with the chances of war – this may prove a better defence against the storm and the tempest than the former ones.

From this ancient and renowned Edifice I took my way towards the School-house, and, as I passed down another street leading to the River Loman I observed a building similar in some respects to the one I had noticed at my entrace into the Town, which was erected AD. 1517 by John Greenway, a rich Woolstapler of the town for 6 poor men and who also endowed it with a revenue of 5^{d} each per week.

At the bottom of this street, which falls to the Loman I passed over the little river by means of a bridge of one arch, and soon after reached the gate of the School house where is a Porters Lodge and by a tablet in its front, I learnt that it was erected by Peter Blundell in 1604 – Aetatis suae 81. There is a large area of near two acres within the walls, at the S.W. end of which is the Schoolhouse, and the houses of the Masters.

The next morning being Sunday I attended divine service at the Old Church: the internal structure and disposition is well proportioned and might have been elegant, had it been seated with any uniformity – over the Pulpit was painted in large characters the first verse of the 58th chapter of Isaiah "Cry aloud! Spare not! Lift up thy voice like a trumpet and shew my people their transgression." The organ had a handsome appearance, possessing most sweet and full tone, and was very well played on without any jig ad libitums a la coutume of the organists in most churches.

This town has been long noted for its Woollen Manufactory and there are at present 1000 looms, nearly 700 in daily use; about 200 combers constantly employed and the returns of trade are about £150,000 per annum.

After Church I mounted my horse and repassing the Bridge which consisted of 5 arches over the Exe which is here 136 feet wide and was built AD. 1570 chiefly by the munificence of Mr Walter Tyrell a mercer of the town who also left a fund for its support – I turned to the left and skirting the River I observed on its opposite side Collypriest once a seat of the Blundells. It was seated in a hollow between two hills, clad with wood, and had a pleasing appearance.

The road for three miles were extremely pleasant, the hills were charmingly wooded and the subjacent meadows seem as if they were an eternal verdure.

At Bickleigh bridge, 3 miles, I diverted from the Exeter Road, taking one on the right for Thorverton which after I had passed by Fursdon a seat of a gentlemen of the same name I entered. This, a mean straggling town I rode through and at the five mile stone from Exeter was struck by the size of an oak, whose circumference at two feet from the ground I found to be 21 feet.

Soon after I passed Upton Pyne Church decorated in the richest style and several antique figures in bas relief on the turret of the tower.

Pynes the seat of Sir Stafford Northcote, within the last ten years has undergone very great changes and by the modern style of improvement has been shewn off to wonderful advantage.

A short way brought me to the River Creedy over which I passed by a bridge, and on an eminence near the junction of this stream with the Exe I observed the new-built House of a Mr. Jackson. That space and extent of ground, which give consequence to a Gentleman's Country seat are here wanting, but if these can be overlooked there is an ample compensation in the prospect either as seen in the more sequestered walks of a hanging wood reflected in the Creedy, or in the

J. Gendall del.t

PYNES,

THE SEAT OF SIR STAFFORD NORTHCOTE, BAR.T

more and enlarged scale as viewed from the windows.

Passing into the public road, I kept strait on, leaving the Bridge which conducted to Exeter on my left. The way now ran parallel to the River and from the more elevated parts afforded a number of delightful views.

By means of this wear which spreads itself across the whole River, a considerable portion of its waters, is separated and conducted to several Mills, which at Exweek (a small hamlet) in particular are employed in the serge manufactory. Beyond the meadow land which occupies the whole level tract and on the other side of the River, the country rises and on its aclivity is ornamented with a number of Villa's beautifully set off by rows and groves of fine Elms – and as soon as the Exe arrives within view of the Walls of Exeter, it again begins to be employed in the manufactures of the City. These mills are chiefly for scouring, stamping or pressing the Serges and other sorts of cloths, giving them at the same time their whiteness and closeness of texture. The building behind the Mills is an Edifice wherein moves the Engine that forces the waters through pipes for the supply of the city. By this diversion of a considerable portion of water from the River, a large tract of land is surrounded, which is called the Island on which besides the Buildings for the Manufactures there are a number of handsome houses.

Having now crossed the Oakhampton, and soon after the Moreton turnpike roads, I past before Franklin, a seat of Counsellor Fanshawes, embosomed in groves of noble Elms: and soon after reached Cowicke, an old House that came from the Speke Family to the present Proprietor Counsellor White. This is an ancient Edifice, and is either a part of, or founded on the site, of a Priory, which before the Dissolution, was a cell to the Abbey of Tavistock.

On the Northern side of this House is a grove of uncommonly large Elms, and indeed throughout the grounds and in every hedge between them and Exeter this charming tree is seen, in the highest luxuriance and plenty. Through a break amid the successive ranges of Elms, Exeter is beheld, with its turreted Cathedral, rising with lordly grandeur over the subjacent city.

A ridge of half a mile brought me before a handsome house, the residence of Mrs. Honeywood, and soon after to the Cross of Alphington.

Alphington is a pleasant village – the public road that passes through, being decorated on both its sides with a succession of neat villas. The clergymans in an especial manner attracts the attention: the front of this however is open only to the Exminster road, which diverges from the turnpike at the church. In this Edifice the only curious object is the Font, and this is certainly worthy of notice on account of its Antique appearance. At the end of this Village the road divides: the one on the right leading through Chudleigh and Ashburton to Plymouth and the other on the left to the same Place through Newton and Totness. On this latter my way ran: and after the space of near a mile brought me before the House and lawn of Peamore, which though from an intersection by the road it loses a good deal of its compactness, is yet a spot of no common beauty.

Passing before the gates of Kenbury, late the seat of R. Cooke Esq., through the Villages of Kenford and Kenn, and by a delightful winding valley, to my house at Oxton the 13th of September, the space of ten days having been most pleasantly whiled away in this little tour to the Northern parts of the County.

Tiverton had a population of about 8,000 in 1850 and had already prospered not only as a market town but for manufacture of woollens and lace. Heathcotes and Co purchased a woollen mill in the town in 1815 and started a profitable association with the town that is continuing still. The firm has large modern buildings and only the gates and gatehouses of the original buildings remain.

Even Tiverton's production of wool and serges fell between 1800 and 1850 although the introduction of a large lace manufactory had reduced the effect of unemployment. A market was regularly held in the town and a new market building completed in 1850 is still used.

At the top of St. Peters Street is the Parish Church and nearby Tiverton Castle. The Church is built of red stone with parts of Beer stone, and each of the cobbled paths across the churchyard are flanked by yews trimmed and shaped like nine pins. Much of the worn Tudor carving being restored relates to John Greenway who was a patron of the church, and a wealthy wool merchant. The carved ships that form a central part of the stonework represent armed merchantmen of the time when Greenway used to import wool and wine and export woollen goods. The nearby castle, with its stone circular tower and fragmented walls is open to the public from time to time during the summer.

The almshouses mentioned in the diary are still used for housing the elderly, but those at the start of St. Peters Street no longer have an uninterupted view to the River but are faced by the former Chilcott Free school building. The National School, a good stone building which was completed in 1844 and now houses the local museum stands only a short way

W. H. Bartlett. W. Taylor

COLLIPRIEST HOUSE, ON THE RIVER EXE, NEAR TIVERTON.

FISHER, SON, & Co LONDON. 1830.

from the old site of the Borough Gaol and House of Correction which were built only two years later. Most of the Gaol and the House of Correction has been demolished but the front part has been converted to two houses by the Devon Historic Buildings Trust.

A late Victorian town hall, massively handsome, at the top of St. Andrew Street is close to the Church of St. Georges, a mellow stone structure finished in 1730. Most of the old buildings have been substantially altered in the town centre, but the ancient Blundell's buildings have been usefully converted to flats, with the School housed in more modern ones on the Sampford Peverell road to the East of the town.

The Exe Valley is one of the most attractive in the County, and its undulating hills and billowing deciduous plantations, which in the autumn are a colourful delight, stretch on to Bickleigh Bridge where there is an attractive group of cob and thatched buildings.

By 1845 a branch line of the railway reached the town and a canal, which had been started in 1810 linked it to Taunton, and carried fertilizers, corn and lime. The Grand Western Canal, used commercially until around 1920, has been restored between Tiverton and Canonsleigh and is used as a country park. It is well used around Tiverton whence a horse-drawn barge operates for the benefit of tourists, and between Sampford Peverell and Canonsleigh it is a remote refuge for wildlife.

Upton Pyne, only a couple of miles from Cowley Bridge which was built in 1813, was until recently nothing larger than a few white rendered and slate or thatched houses straggling by the Parish Church of St. Peter. Recently it has started to expand. In 1850 the whole parish had 550 living in it and was under the patronage of the Northcote family who lived at Pynes, which was a small brick house, but which a year later was rebuilt in magnificent style.

Exwick was a suburb of the City; Alphington had 1250 people in the parish in 1850, with a National School and the thriving church of St. Michaels.

TIVERTON — *From Skrinkhills*

South East View of the CASTLE of TIVERTON in the County of Devon. Anno 1730.

Engraved by Thomas, for Dunsford's Historical Memoirs of Tiverton, Anno 1790.

3. East Devon

by the Reverend John Swete

In the pleasant summer of 1794, John Swete, accompanied by a servant, rode through parts of East Devon, and says of Ottery St. Mary:

From the very picturesque scenes on the banks of the river Otter, I regained the town by the suburbs where the Manufactory had been erected; and passing its front, pursued my walk up Mill Street, and soon arrived opposite the house, once the residence of Sir Walter Raleigh.

..... one part, that beyond the gateway is inhabited, the rest being open in its windows, and dilapidated – and to my enquiries, who might be the tenant I learnt that a butcher now occupied the rooms which had once been graced by the brightest ornament of the County.

The next morning about ten I quitted Ottery which in its buildings, excepting those surrounding the Church has little to attract notice, and peeping over the bridge near the Wear which I visited the preceeding evening, the road brought me in front of "Cadhay" which was separated from it only by a single field.

It will be seen to be an edifice of no common note – it conveys to the spectator an idea of former consequence, and I looked with some degree of reverence on the groves that surround it.

By 1850, Ottery St. Mary had grown by a thousand to 3,500, but no doubt remained the well paved town described in the Journal. Raleigh's house was destroyed by fire in 1805 and a handsome brick property took its place and is still there today. The Coleridge family were important landowners and the poet was born here in 1772. Cadhay, a fine Elizabethan mansion is now open to the public. The Church Corporation Trust ran the local Grammar School – The Kings School, and in addition to the magnificent church of St. Mary there were Independant and Wesleyan chapels. The attractive Georgian buidings close to the Church and the tumbling wear have survived the years and the recent considerable growth. From Ottery St. Mary he passed by Talaton and then on to Payhembury.

Two miles from Coldstock, by a rugged stoney road and steep ascent, I joined the turnpike leading from Cullompton to Honiton, and being now on a common by a winding track of greensward among the heath, and which originally seemed to have been the chief entrace to the entrenchment from the road below, which is reputed to have been Roman and called as such, Cockenhay Street, I made my approach to Hembury Fort, perhaps one of the strongest and most commanding stations in the Country. Through three passes over which rose as many high and steep vallas I passed to the Encampment which had been formed to the south west extremity of that very elevated common, which appeared to be a part of the Blackdown thrusting itself out in a point over the grounds which lay at a vast depth below.

The Fort is of an oval form, deriving its figure from that of the promontory. In the time of the Romans, or their successors this castle must have been impregnable, it is so strongly fortified even by Nature itself on every quarter but the North as to preclude attack, and even there were two very high vallas and deep passes which must have given a besieged army within encamped the greatest security. I began my view with the town and delightful valley of Honiton. Beneath me, were Buckerell Hills, beyond, in a vale clad with woodland and sheltered by high hills was seated "Combe" an old mansion of the Putts. Near this were perceived the windings of the Otter which as a silver serpent rolled itself through a most enchanting expanse of greenest pastures, to the town, to which it lends its name, whose collegiate towers rise high over its surrounding groves, and "crowned the glade".

After a three mile traverse on the Down, throughout the whole, uncertain where to steer for the Abbey of Dunkeswell I at length descried a cart, and hurrying towards it, from the driver I got certain information. Taking my course now due North I reached an inclosed track and found myself in the road that lead from Wolford Lodge, the seat of Colonel Simcoe, to Dunkeswell Church. Accosting a lad of 15 or 16, I asked for Dunkeswell, and was told it lay somewhat below in the valley.

"Was the Abbey there?"

"What? D'ye mean the old ruins?"

"Yes"

"Oh no! They were two miles further down."

"Two mile" cried I, "from whence?"

"Why from the City of Dunkeswell!"

"Were these ruins worth seeing?"

"I don't know, not I, they be a ragged set of old houses."

Finding that the road was very ragged also, my curiosity began sensibly to abate, for it was now between 2 and 3 O'clock and the heat of the day was intense. After a short pause however I persisted and descending a steep hill that ended in a narrow morassy bottom, through which ran a clear and beautiful stream, I entered Dunkeswell Church town, of the more elevated phrase of the lad, Dunkeswell City, which to my mortification, for I was in hopes of being able to procure refreshment at the place, I found it consisted of half a dozen miserable hovels, among which were a small chapel – looking Church with a diminutive spire. From a poor meagre smith, whose anvil looked rusty from want of use, I had confirmation of the lad's intelligence that it was two miles to the Abbey, that the road was exceedingly bad, that I must return the same way, and that there was not a post house in the parish. . . . . . I pushed on to the Abbey, and woefully experienced the truth of the Smith's observations. Only the dilapidated walls of the Abbey remain . . . there appeared in the whole assemblage with the surrounding scenery of trees and rivulet, somewhat of the picturesque, though the buildings in themselves were uncommonly mean and insignificant. On alighting from my horse to explore further I was in an instance encircled by a little host of children and females, whose tattered garments and meagre looks betrayed a "variety of wretchedness".

During my circuit of the ruins I had dispatched my servant to a neighbouring Mill and Farmhouses, in quest of bread and cheese, and in particular to procure a feed of corn for the poor horses who had been on the road from 10 to 4. Neither of these however being to hand I remounted and got away from this region of want as fast as the hills and stoney roads would permit."

I pursued my way to Honiton between flourishing plantations of larch and within a quarter mile again entered on a common where the road from Dunkeswell lost itself in that of the turnpike leading from Taunton to Honiton. On the right of this the common had been enclosed! The hedges were of considerable height and width, and they were planted in the middle with beach and at the edges with willows, these last consisted of stakes, and were sprouting in great luxuriance, superadded to this was a wattled fence of dry wood, black thorn, etc.

Dumpton Hill, rising abrupt on every side from the plain to an immense height. I soon after marked the village of Combe Raleigh, whose Church surrounded by several neat houses wore an appearance extremely picturesque.

Hembury Fort is a magnificent viewing point and recently excavations have reaffirmed that it was originally an Iron Age fort and later used by the Romans. The Blackdown Hills are eight miles to the north beyond Culmstock and Hemyock marking the border of Devon and Somerset, but Hembury Fort is not related to them.

Dunkeswell parish church, St. Nicholas, was rebuilt in 1817, and again in 1865/8. In 1850 there was a neat Wesleyan chapel and a School House as well as a beer seller called Willie Edward in the village. Today it has the charm of a working village dependant on farming, with a sparkling stream and a number of pleasant thatched cottages and too much corrugated iron, although progress has added a pub!

The fragmentary remains of Dunkeswell Abbey are still reached by the steep sunken narrow road described, although the nearby properties are neat and attractive. Mrs. Simcoe built a church in the Abbey grounds in 1842 which remains in good repair with some excellent carving.

Collegiate Church of Ottery St. Mary, Devon.

I entered the east end of the town of Honiton, having rode almost through it, at length finished my days journey at the Golden Lion.

Honiton chiefly consists of one wide street East and West, and it has been so indebted to fires which have laid waste the ancient buildings, that was it not for the market place which stands in the midst and which is uncommonly mean, would be considered handsome. It has a chapel called Allhallows at its eastern end but the Church which was erected in the year 1480 or thereabouts, by Peter Courtenay Bishop of Exeter, stands half a mile southwards on the site of a steep hill, to which the approach is both disagreeable and inconvenient. From the summit of this Hill descends the turnpike road from London to Exeter and throughout the whole of the declevity the eye of the traveller finds no intermission of delight. The whole country spread out before it in one continuous vale bounded on the North and South by natural barriers of immense hills, which run towards the West in parallel lines, terminating in the Northern quarter in the promontary of Hembury Fort. The landscape that fills up the intermediate space is diversified with all the beauties that can be displayed by intermixture of corn and pasture. The low valley and gently swelling knoll, the town, the villages, and the numerous seats which with the grove and lawn, add the grace of elegance to the more uncultured beauties of nature.

Gittisham which had a neat trim appearance and was most charmingly situated in a rich well wooded valley, having forded a little river which descended from the neighbouring hills, I passed through a grove of venerable elms casting a solemn shade, impervious to the sun and alighted at the gate of the school house. The civil master of which soon joined me with the key of the Church.

[*Travelling on to Netherton in Farway he observed*]

This fair house of Netherton which Sir Edmond Prideaux built, though no longer fair, is the place of residence of his lineal successor Sir Wilmot, and with him it bids fair to fall to the grounds, for the mansion and the family will probably perish together, they both totter and to neither is their a prop of support.

Approaching Colyton in a little open plain watered by a rivulet I had a pleasing view of the Church, rising high on the North part of the town. The tower was of a singular construction. The lower part was square and very probably the whole of the original building, from this rose another of an octagonal form and terminating conically. This as at Ottery St. Mary was placed in the centre of the church.

Quitting Colcombe Castle I rode up a long and steep hill to the North to the new house of Shute. This was erected, or rather begun in 1787 by the present representative of the Pole Family who in the year 1789, by the king's permission took himself the name of de la Pole . . . . the South front is of good height being of four storeys and the site chosen for the prospect which it commanded, in the utmost perfection the rich and finely wooded valley are expanded to the East and West, and terminated in the villages of Axmouth and Seaton.

From Shute by a long and steep assent without windings conducted direct up the face of the hill strew'd over with pointed flints, as large and rough as they were taken from their beds. I gained the summit of Shute hill and from this eminence the views were inconceivably fine.

In passing over the common, the rough road descending the whole way I had a pleasing command of the North and East country, the seat of the late Lady Drake, Willmenton, Axminster and a sweet pastoral valley watered by the Rivers Yarte and Axe.

About eight I entered Axminster, the Church of which as I passed it attracted my notice on account of its Antiquity.

The countryside around Honiton, particularly viewed from the Axminster Road is outstandingly attractive. A neat Gothic style toll house and its gate is at the bottom of the hill from which the panoramic views are seen. The fifty years after Swete's visit saw the towns population rise from 2,300 to over 4,000, although the towns main street with its new houses built after the disastrous fires of 1747 and 1765, remained unaltered. A Market House over a large Public Room was built in 1825, and the gas Works was constructed in 1835, the lace making industry had declined against cheap competition producing an inferior commodity and by 1850 the Honiton Bank had failed. Above all the Parliamentary Reform Act of 1832 had especial significance for the town which was one of the worst examples of a rotten borough in the country. It had a pottery, and in addition a tannery, a brewery, and iron foundry three corn mills, several malt kilns, and four chapels as well as a new parish church – St. Pauls, adjacent Allhallows Chapel. In spite of the woeful predictions about Netherton it is now an attractive property, although without the thriving Deer Park.

Engraved by W. Cooke from a drawing by J.S. Cotman for the Beauties of England and Wales.

GATEWAY TO SHUTE HOUSE.
Devonſhire.

London Published by Vernor & Hood, Poultry, July 1803.

Drawn by T. H. Shepherd. Engraved by H. Wallis.

COLYTON CHURCH, DEVONSHIRE.

The next morning, with Mrs. Swete who with my two eldest children had joined me, I set off in the chaise for Ford Abbey.

All the sensations of disappointment and toil were however recompensed in the amplest manner by the pleasure we received on our arrival at Ford Abbey. The approach and the contiguous grounds in a picturesque light are most striking they are in the old style.

Though erected at periods far distant of each other, the more modern buildings of the Prideaux's incorporated with the ancient ones of the Abbey, yet there was a unison that pervaded the whole Pile. All wore the garb of Antiquity, and all was uncommonly attractive, the carving of stone which was a yellowish free stone, the pillars and balustrades produced an exceedingly fine effect, not less striking on account of the elegance and richness of the decorations than for their venerable magnificence. In the central tower which rose high with ornamental mouldings was the chief entrance, and this as well as the rest of the edifice was created with battlements.

[*Returning to Axminster he then explored towards Musbury.*]

I passed into the grounds of Ash, and soon reached the house which though it had been a place of consequence from the time of William the Conquerer, till within the last 20 years, the major part of which it had been the possession and residence of the Drake family, seemed to have met its fate. Its grandeur was gone perhaps for ever and the seat itself, having passed by sale into the hands of some tradesmen at Axminster, was now degraded to a farm house.

The next morning proving raining we were detained in this town till noon. As we were however in a good inn, the George, with many obliging people and excellent accommodation we judged ourselves not unfortunate, and to while away the time not unpleasantly or unprofitably, under the shelter of umbrellas we sallied forth to the Carpet Manufactory.

Here we were received and had every attention paid us by the proprietor Mr. Whitley. Conducted through several rooms we had the pleasure of beholding the whole operation from the apartment and winding the worsted, which consisted of innumeable shades of every colour, and which was in the hands of children, to the perfection of the carpet, the beauty and elegance of which and of course the price, depended, on the variety of pattern, its size and excellence of workmanship. Of those women, for females were the sole artists, on a piece of great expense and elegance nothing that I can conceive, could be superior to their adroitness. Here we passed an hour.

From Axminster, passed up over wild and bleak downs, without a single object to engage the eye. Not a tree, nor a dell to be seen till within a mile or two of the sea, when we skirted, after a deep delve into the valley of Uplyme, the lower part of its village. The church standing on a small eminence at the upper end, and appearing a rather pleasing object.

On entering the town (Lyme), the descent became more rapid falling through a very decent wide street to the sea, and at the bottom very near the shore, we came to our inn, the Three Cups.

Whilst our dinner was preparing we walked from the Rooms to the fortifications which seemed to possess strength enough to defend the town from the plunder of privateer. At this place was a pleasant walk, on a flat pavement, and a shed covered for the reception of company, over which several houses towered, and in an intermediate space waved the Tamerisk its branches of a pale green, producing a most charming effect.

A narrow footway conducted us to the bathing machines, and further still to the pier or Cobb as it is termed. At this spot the view of the Town and Cliffs beyond it was uncommonly fine and romantic, the sloping ridge on which the house and church arose had a fine relief given it by the falling hill, and the Cliffs, behind, which dipped diagonally and were, in seeing, strata of lead colour, marle or clay. The whole of this scenery was an intermixture of the Picturesque and Romantic, overhung by the mountainous heights, the town was conspicuously beautiful.

Lyme however, from the cursory observations that I had been able to make, did not strike me as being an eligible place for Summer resort, for the country circumjacent was very hilly, it was void of trees, it had no picturesque scenery, no rides, no diversity of walks. The shore, when the tide had not far receeded was pebbly, of course neither well adapted for bathing, exercise or amusement.

Passing from Lyme towards Seaton I had a good view of Stedcombe house, the seat of the Reverend Hollwell Hallet. It rose well, as a large brick building, lofty and of a squre figure, and seemed detached from all offices, for no other structure was discernible. A most noble clump of magnificent elms towered high in front, shrouding it often from the sight, and before it appeared a small village.

Passing the handsome bridge at Colyford, I rode through the village, however mean it may now be, in earlier time of no small consequence. Of this place was Sir Thomas Gates, though of the lowest extraction, won fame in the Netherlands, knighted by James Ist and after became Governor of Virginia where it was supposed he died.

Drawn by G.B. Campion from a sketch by Lady Romilly

Engraved by Thos. Higham,

FORD ABBEY DEVON

THE SEAT OF ____ GWYNNE ESQ. TO WHOM THIS PLATE IS MOST RESPECTFULLY INSCRIBED
BY THE PROPRIETORS

A mile and a half brought us to Seaton, a small village consisting chiefly of one little street which opened on the beach, composed of pebbles.

Seaton amidst the rage for bathing on the western coast, was now beginning to have its share of company, chosen at first for cheapness and retirement. Thus has every place of summer resort, from obscurity to progressive advancement to elegance and expense throughout the whole coast from Weymouth to Torbay risen to celebrity. Teignmouth, Dawlish, Exmouth have been what Seaton is, and in no remote period I doubt not that Seaton will vie with either of them. for though it has little extent of beach, and that bad, yet between high mountainous hills it has a sheltered situation, and the environs in point of picturesque beauty and varied rides, are equal if not superior to most on the coast. The Inn in the village is but small, but is unusually neat, possessing very good accommodation and civil people.

Both Ford Abbey and Lyme Regis were within easy reach of Axminster and deserved a visit, as they still do. Both are now within Dorsetshire although Ford Abbey is in the parish of Thorncombe, and in 1800 this detached parish was in the Axminster Hundred and part of Devon, to be annexed to Dorsetshire in 1842, when Dalwood and Stockland detached parishes of Dorsetshire were annexed to Devonshire.

Ford Abbey is open to the public, and Lyme Regis has grown considerably to become a popular holiday resort, the charm of the steeply sloping high Street, the Cobb and the Three Cups in Broad Street are a reminder of those early days.

The George Hotel in Axminster stands imposingly in the centre, and the old coaching inn still caters for travellers in a very acceptable way. The centre is itself an attractive place with the Church, the old Carpet Factory building, and a pleasant assortment of stone built Georgian or Early Victorian properties and open market stalls. By 1850 the town had grown to around 3,000 and the celebrated carpet factory had closed in 1835, although another has opened in more recent times. In 1836 a workhouse was built and later enlarged for up to 400 paupers. There had been a postal service for some years before the introduction of stamps in 1841, and bigger places like Axminster had had a Post Office where daily mail could be dispatched for many years. Colyford and Axmouth are mentioned and curiously their relative merits remain the same. Colyford which is not as seedy now as it was around 1800, has nevertheless suffered from the effects of motor cars and other vehicles rumbling through it on the coast road, whilst Axmouth is an attractive small village enjoying the beauty and wildlife of the Seaton marshes, a magnificent wild setting which has probably hardly changed over the years. Stedcombe, converted for holiday use, is set on a hillside amongst the same wooded and pastoral surrounds. Ashe house is also unchanged.

Seaton as predicted, became a holiday resort by 1850 with some 760 people living here compared with Beer where there were 1,200. Seaton is now the larger of the two (in 1981, 4975 to Beer's 1316) and has the atmosphere of brash modernity whilst Beer, because of its setting maintains some exclusiveness. Both have developed relatively recently.

Beer Harbour

Having slept here, we entered Beer, a small town consisting of one street which terminated in a pebbly strand. The scenery around this place was bold and romantic, the cliffs in particular hovering high, whilst the fishing boat passing from or entering the cove with its white sail, arresting a beam of light whilst scudding beneath the shaded rock, was productive of one of the most pleasing affecting that a water view can afford. Some of the houses in Beer being built of freestone from the neighbouring quarries had a decent appearance and many of their

Drawn by G.B. Campion. SIDMOUTH, DEVON. Engraved by James Bingley.

fronts were decorated in the most charming manner by myrtles, in high bloom and luxuriance, which perfumed the air with their delicate odours.

[*Leaving Beer and passing by the nearby quarries, describing the beauty of the stone he continues.*]

I came to the Quarry mouth, at this sight I was exceedingly surprised, for not having had any previous intimation of what I was to see, I had pictured to myself immense rocks, which by the labour of ages had received the form of cliffs, of vast height and unusual magnificance. What then was my disappointment when I beheld the mouth of a cave only before me. Miners lighting up their farthing candles proposed to conduct us through the subteranean.

From the quarry the Sidmouth road was extremely good ... a sudden break or division made them remarkable forming that singular chasm which from all the high grounds, west of the Exe is particularly discernable and is known by the appellation of Sidmouth gap.

At the foot of a long descent, through a narrow track of pastures winded the little River Sid, and where it crossed the road a bridge of two arches rose over it. This is a very picturesque scene, the elevated arch over the chief part of the stream was very handsome.

The village beyond, rich overhanging elms, the vista of road, and the distant conical hill, when thus beheld combined together were unusually attractive and produced a most pleasing effect, this was Sidford. In this street was a Pothouse of a more decent appearance than ordinary, kept by one Ball, late servant, as the public were informed in large letters, to Sir J. De la Pole Bart. As we passed under the sign of the Blue Ball, the landlord was standing at his door seemingly expectant that we might bait at this house, on our moving on however, if I might hazard a pun, I thought that the sign became a mere expressive symbol, for it struck me that Mr. Ball looked blue.

At the end of the village of Sidford we turned from the Exeter Road, passing down the valley, till we reached Sidmouth.

Having passed through the town we approached the sea, and within a few houses of the end of the street which opened onto the beach, came to the London Inn, where the Rooms are, and where we met with excellent accommodation. As we had two or three hours to dinner we strolled to reconnoitre, and having seen the major part of the town, we went directly to the mall, an artificial walk on the beach, carried parallel with and in front of the sea. Before a shed, well constructed, with seats sheltered from the weather, but open to the prospect was a handsome billiard room seemingly well frequented. This beautiful walk ran, and extended itself nearly to the western most cliff: from it however was a little dip to a rivulet, over which was a foot bridge, and immediately beyond, the Bathing machines, a cottage or two for fishermen, had been raised under the cliff, their boats were drawn on shore in front, their nets were hung to dry on poles. The cliff itself was of a ruddy tint, fringed and overhung with brush wood, ivy, grass, and a large mass of it, which was daily diminished by the buffeting of the waves yet stood amid the water. Behind the cliff were stakes and poles for fixing nets to take fish at high water, and at the ebb of the tide.

Sidmouth is the gayest place of resort on the Devon coast and every elegancy, every luxury, every amusement is here to be met with – iced creams, milliners shops, cards, billiards, plays, circulation libraries, attract notice in every part, and as I saw a smart gentleman take a novel from his pocket in the public shed, I presume such to be the fashion of the place.

About five we took our departure, passing by the Mall and in front of a handsome row of buildings, that was rising in a field open to the sea, a speculation. From the excellence of the houses and there pleasant exposure their scheme will be successful.

The Beer stone quarries have been worked since Roman times, and are in production today. Today there is an open sided quarry, but on the opposite side of the minor road to the workings visited by Swete. His lengthy description of quarrying remarks on the ability of the miners to work in such dimly lit caves and the kiln for making agricultural lime in front. The stone is mainly used for agricultural lime, although recently the repairs to Exeter Cathedral have engendered a fresh demand for building stone.

The fishermen of both Beer and Sidmouth follow the tradition of selling their wares from close to the beach they sail from, to the benefit of everyone, although modern boats and not sailing vessels are now used.

The growth of Sidmouth from 1800 to 1850 was large and during this time it changed rapidly; the numerous elegant terraces and villas and a new Market house were built. By 1838, an enlarged and improved promenade had been completed, and plans were entertained for the construction of a harbour, which mercifully was not pursued. All Saints was built in 1839, the Independant Chapel erected in 1846, both after the Wesleyan Chapel of 1837. The Gas Works, the beacon of progress, was established in 1837, and the Water Works in 1845. Education was not neglected, with a large National School, connected with the parish church, All Saints Church School built by subscription in 1848 and a British School commenced in the same year. During these years the elegance of Sidmouth was firmly established.

THE OLD PANNIER BRIDGE, SIDFORD

W. H. Bartlett. P. Heath.

THE YORK HOTEL, AND LIBRARY, SIDMOUTH.

PETER JACKSON, LONDON & PARIS.

We reached Otterton. This is a very pleasant village, surrounded by arable grounds on every quarter but the West, where the River Otter winds through rich meadows, washing the outskirts of the village. On a rising ground just above the stream, stands the Mansion House, and the Church, being contiguous to one another, and in the period before the dissolution, from the Nunnery, which stood on the site of the present house, it is supposed there was an immediate communication, from one of its rooms into the chancel.

Separated from Otterton by a pasture or two lying to the North West is Bicton, one of the many seats in the County possessed by Dennis Rolle Esq. About the latter end of the 16th Century was a mansion house built, to which was annexed a Deer Park and in process of time fine gardens, ornamented with slopes, terraces and parallelogram ponds, after the absurd fashion of the times.

The Old mansion of Sir Robert Dennis has been demolished and a new one begone, on a higher site more northwards in the Park, of this however the two wings, which were to project from the chief edifice, were only completed and they yet remain in the same unfinished state. The chief embellishment of its situaton arises from the magnificent and venerable trees which surround it, the Beech in particular being as fine as are to be met with in any part of the Kingdom.

Within a short distance from hence we passed through the village of East Budleigh not far from which in the road to Exmouth is Tidwell, in former ages the seat of the St. Cleers. The present building however is the third on record of less standing than a century, and is now remarkable for nothing but the large and beautiful Myrtles that spread themselves nearly over the whole front.

But Hayes that lies on the western part of the Parish would demand more attention from the curious stranger, as being the birth-place of Sir Walter Raleigh. Here this great man, amongst any of the worthies who have given honour to the County was born A.D.1552.

From the village of East Budleigh, near which is the Parish Church, I turned from the public road to the left and having pursued a track direct South for somewhat more than a mile, I reached the Western shore of the little bay formed by the sand bank at the Otter mouth, having by too quick a turn to the left missed the road to the village of Budleigh Salterton which I was in quest of, I had now to pursue my way on a shore of pebbles, into which my horse sunk to the knee. I dismounted, and had as disagreable a walk of an half mile, for so far had I got to the East of Budleigh, as can be imagined.

At last I gained the village, but found little compensation for my toil. The view of the coast was extensive, but then it was composed of the loosest pebbles, and there was scarce a house that fronted it. The buildings in general of the meanest cast, intermingling with trees had a picturesque appearance, but in other respects, had so few of those points requisite for a watering place that I think its improvement, in equipping a few cottages for invalids have been carried nearly to their full extent.

HAYE'S FARM, EAST BUDLEIGH,
DEVONSHIRE.
The Birthplace of Sir Walter Raleigh.

The men are farmers and fishermen, and the women lace makers, and the natural production which for some years past have rendered the place well known, are its fine lobsters and its laver. This last under the class of mosses, is a vegetable growing on the rocks, and for its flavour is in high request at the tables of many.

I pursued my way to Exmouth. The roads from hence, and indeed they had been so for some time, were bad, and dangerous to the horses from the abundance of loose pebbles with which they were strewed. This seems to be the stratum of which the whole ridge from the eminence at Woodbury encampment to the hills rising above Exmouth, consists.

T. Allom. Wm Le Petit.

BICTON-HOUSE, DEVONSHIRE.

THE SEAT OF JOHN ROLLE, BARON ROLLE, TO WHOM THIS PLATE IS MOST RESPECTFULLY DEDICATED BY THE PUBLISHERS.

The Inn at the Place or square, was encompassed by the Old Town, sheltered by the South East hill from the sea and open only to the River. In front of the most Western range of houses grew a line of fine branching elms, and the view from this shady promenade, here by successive buildings it became shut out, was enchanting. At the flow of the River the wide waste of mud and sand were covered, and an expanse of water, on whose surface floated their port vessels laden with their cargoes, was bordered by a tract of country which for variety and beauty for landscape might rarely be exceeded. This was that Exmouth to which about 20 years ago Invalids from the several parts of the County resorted, the other watering places on the coast now so much in repute, were then scarcely known.

As the fame of Exmouth increased so did its buildings. It was not now merely sought for by the Invalid, but was considered during the Summer months, as an eligible retreat for the children of idleness and gaiety. To those the hill intervening between the town and the sea was in request, and building gradually connected the eminence with the plain. About fourteen years since a neat chapel was built in the midway, and in 1792, a range of brick houses commenced on the Hill.

From one of these houses it was possible to see the headland of Babbicombe, up the River Exe and across to the Warren, the village of Starcross, where was the mooring place of those vessels, colliers in particular whose tonnage precluded any further advance up the estuary, Mamhead, the Castle of Powderham, Belvidere Haldown,

Lawrence Tower, Exeter Cathedral, Topsham and a variety of villages.

After breakfast next morning we departed, the carriage road ran parallel to the River pursuing that which conducted to Exeter, till within two miles of the City when turning to the West, it crossed the Exe by Countess Wear bridge, and proceeding by Exminster and Kenton to Oxton.

A shorter and pleasanter way, cutting off at least one half of the distance, lay by the Ferry at or near the mouth of the Exe, the boat of which is also accommodated to the conveyance of wheeled carriages. On the opposite shore rises a high ridge of drifted sand tufted with long spiny grass, this thrusts itself about half a mile or less in bredth, having one side the River and on the other the sea. This track, from the rabbits that for many years were kept on it, is called the Warren.

Both Otterton and East Budleigh remain delightful small villages, and change, until recently, has been very slow. Today the same streams and the smell of local baked bread at Otterton, would be as familiar as they were a century or two ago like the Elizabethan buildings in their main streets. The delightful carving in St. Mary's church at East Budleigh, especially of the Raleigh pew, with their crest and date 1537, are worth seeing.

Bicton House was not completed until near the end of the 18th Century although much of the garden and grounds were laid out before. The new Bicton church was completed in 1850. Tidwell House stands beside the B 5178 and is now a guest house, and Bicton House is an agricutural college.

White's Directory *states that "Budleigh Salterton has risen from a few straggling fishing huts, into a fashionable watering place, during the present century. The shops and inns form one principal street . . ." This growth has left an indelible impression on a town that has almost doubled from about 2,400*

EXMOUTH — *From Louisa Terrace.*

then to 4,400 a century later. By 1850 it had become an attraction for the lovers of natural history in seeking moss agate, jasper, and other rich pebbles yielded from amongst the flat stones of the beach. James Lackington, a London bookseller had built the Wesleyan chapel in 1811, and Holy Trinity Church had followed in 1812, a National School had been paid for in 1842 by Lord Rolle, and it had two circulating libraries and reading rooms.

At Exmouth ships took on pilots for Topsham, and Turf lock at the entrance to the Exeter canal. The evident expansion around 1800 continued and there was still further development including some of the most magnificent properties in the town, Louisa, Trefusis, and Beacon terraces, on Beacon Hill, Adelaide terrace and Church terrace. Four chapels were built during the period, and Holy Trinity Church was constructed in 1824/5. Lord Rolle had been responsible for this, and also for a number of other public works including the Market House in 1830, the plantation and walks beneath the Beacon and the sea wall in 1842. The town attracted a good number of wealthy families to live in the new and large houses built there, and patronise the Public Rooms on the Beacon or reading rooms at Sheppards walk. Like Sidmouth there was the Honiton lace industry to provide some employment, and a wide variety of fish were caught in the Estuary. Today no more than a dozen full time fishermen operate from Exmouth whilst in 1850 about 300 men and boys made a living from it. The continuous and rapid growth has diminished the overall impact of the Georgian and Regency building, but the Beacon imports a whisper of its ancient elegance. Its attraction as a holiday resort is still very evident.

BUDLEIGH SALTERTON.

4. Exeter

by Lady Paterson

A useful thumb nail sketch is given of Exeter in 1810 in Risdon's Survey of Devon.

> *The City, which is of itself a county, must be considered the capital of Devonshire, where the assizes and all the county meetings are held. The number of houses in 1801, was 3,208, and the population 20,305, of whom 14,300 were returned as being employed in trade and manufacture. The cathedral, which is the principal ornament of the city, was thoroughly repaired, and beautified in 1763, and in 1766 a beautiful modern painted glass window was put up over the west door. There are also eighteen parish churches in the city. In 1741 a noble hospital for the sick and lame, of the county and city, was erected by Dr. Arnold Clarke, assisted by public subscription, and a general asylum for lunatics has been lately erected, which is supported by voluntary contributions. In short the City has of late years been greatly improved by the erection of new buildings of every description. It is governed by a mayor, 24 aldermen, 4 bailiffs, a recorder, chamberlain, sheriff, town clerk etc. There are 13 companies of corporated trades, who in all public processions, attend the mayor in their gowns, with ensigns of their different trades carried before them. It gives the title of earl to the Cecils, and sends two members to Parliament. The right of election, is in the freemen and freeholders. The market is held on Wednesday and Friday.*
>
> *Heavitree parish is a peculiar one, belonging to the Dean and Chapter of Exeter, annexed to which are the churches of St. Sidwell, and St. David, in Exeter. The manor of Heavitree, after continuing for many generations in the Kelly family, was, in 1773 sold by Arthur Kelly, Esq., to John Baring Esq. of Mount Radford, the present possessor.*

In essence it was an Elizabethan City with some insanitary rows of medieval buildings, until the last quarter of the eighteenth century when the spirit of improvement first became evident. This need to modernise and enthusiasm for it reached into the early nineteenth century and with this momentum there came the reconstitution of many of the institutions as well as the renewal of the fabric of Exeter. With it perished not only slums and antiquated customs, but inevitably the unchanged ways of life which had continued for decades. In 1800 the scale of the City was still reasonably small, of a similar size to present day Barnstaple, and from the heathland of Haldon Hill the traveller could see the separate villages of Alphington, Kenford, Heavitree, Clyst St. Mary, Pinhoe and Wonford. He might as he passed through Exeter have visited Ide, Exwick or Cowley, all of which were small villages quite separate from the town, although by 1850 the spreading houses were starting to stretch out and link with them, a trend that in recent years has been completed.

The sparcity of population around Exeter ensured a splendid rural setting within which the homes of those with wealth exhibited it by the grandeur of their buildings. At a distance whilst travelling up Haldon Hill, the traveller could see Haldon House the home of Sir Lawrence Palk, and to the left Haldon Tower – Castle Lawrence, had been built to honour General Lawrence, and to this day it remains a landmark for most of East Devon. From the top was an extensive view of the City, and Topsham, Lympstone, and Exmouth, on the eastern bank of the Exe. On the west bank was the imposing seat of Lord Courtenay, Powderham Castle, as well as the woods belonging to the Earl of Lisburne, and beyond these the sea. These spectacular views of dimpled hills, trees and much of East Devon are an unchanged delight on a sunny day, although many vantage points which were once open heathland are now parts of Haldon Forest, and mainly coniferous plantations belonging to the Forestry Commission.

Swete's description of Exeter has been destroyed and consequently there is little record of what he thought of the City or its antiquities, although he regularly visited it to meet his friends. There is however a record of a visit he paid to a property called Fordlands to the south of Ide, in which he describes some of the countryside about the City in 1797.

His visit provides a small insight into the countryside around Exeter and the setting of Ide. It was a countryside in a high state of cultivation but frittered into long inclosures which were often hedged by elms which did little to help agriculture. Today the elms have largely gone, as have the many hedges, and the good red soils are cultivated by two or three tractors working on large fields. It was not uncommon to see a kite hovering overhead hunting its prey whilst today only a dozen or so pairs are to be found in South Wales. Fortunately the kestrel is still a common sight hunting along the margins of these "prairie" fields. As he passed down the main street of Ide the villagers were busy at their looms, outworkers for a prosperous industry.

From the higher lands west of Ide where Swete visited so long ago there is a splendid view over Exeter. From here the Cathedral still dominates all that

Pub.d by H. Besley. Directory Office, South St. Exeter.

EXETER CATHEDRAL.

surrounds it, although some of the more modern tower blocks in the shopping centre or the new Devon and Exeter Hospital on Barrack Road stand out as rather incongruous intrusions amongst their domestic surroundings. The old gasometers by the Canal are equally prominent, but the great spread of buildings and the scale of commercial enterprise, have entirely changed what was a well tree'd and attractive landscape, which then seemed more likely to engulf the City with its verdure rather than be lost beneath it.

By 1850 both the prospect and prosperity of the City had changed. Cloth which had dominated the trading and manufacture of both the City and villages about it was less in demand after the Napoleonic Wars. This was possibly the result of the traditional European markets being lost. The East India Company remained a good customer for some years so that even though the trading in Europe declined there was hope for orders from elsewhere. Nevertheless, by 1822, the fall in trade was so great that only 350 hands were employed in the making of serges and other coarse cloth. Three factories were in production at this time, one at Exwick and two on Exe Island.

This undoubted blow to the City's trade seems only to have changed the basis of its prosperity rather than the lasting well being of the place itself. It was still the centre for a great number of trades, and a market town, but perhaps less busy as a port. There was a continuous growth and improvement of housing and other building as the population doubled in the first fifty years of the century to 40,000.

The Old City had been surrounded by a wall and gates with suburbs extending beyond them. Roads were improved and the walls, gates and towers, which had been the hallmark of the medieval town were removed and altered. North Gate was taken down in 1769, East Gate in 1784, West Gate and Quay Gate in 1815, South Gate in 1819, and Broad Gate in 1825. The ancient roadways were improved, although not generally realigned. Gardens and open spaces, orchards and other scraps of land were gradually developed or incorporated for new buildings as old properties were rebuilt.

At this time of change the filthy gaols of the City were removed and the Devon County Gaol and Bridewell, or House of Correction, were completed in 1796 and 1807. The Devon Assize Hall and Session House, now known as "The Castle", were built in 1773 on the site of the old county prison. Good building was common to both public and domestic architecture, which like Bedford Circus, built in 1773 and destroyed during the war time blitz, gave the city considerable dignity. At the turn of the century there were other outstanding terraces like Colleton Crescent and Southernhay.

St. Sidwell, St. Leonards and Heavitree parishes are particularly fortunate to have benefited by the building of some excellent terraces and houses around 1830 which stand today as monuments to good taste, symmetry and the well-to-do middle class of that time. Retired soldiers like General Paterson who leased 4 Park Place in Heavitree, made their homes in the spacious and orderly houses. An insight into the leisured life of the prosperous middle classes in Exeter is glimpsed through the diary of Lady Paterson.

The diary of Lady Paterson records the quiet lives of herself and her family in Exeter during the years 1831 to 1835. The similarity of daily visits and musical practice, trips to town and the theatre, during all these years suggest the apparently slow pace of a stately society, whilst recording comings and goings within the village of Heavitree. Its references, always brief, of the Reform Act of 1832 or the accession of William IV to the throne, place this unassuming record within a National context at a time when the traditional form of society was about to change radically.

Alexander (AGP) and Captain James, sons of Lady Paterson, provide a constant source of regret or anxiety either because they haven't visited or because they have incurred debts. Margaret their daughter is generally referred to as M.M.P. – Miss Margaret Paterson, and her friend Miss Kekewich as Miss K. Lady Paterson's sister Jessy lives in the household and is a maiden aunt, with the apparent virtues of this almost extinct type, and Mr. Caird is the local G.P. who cares for all the minor ailments that ladies of this period enjoyed, as well as the more serious emergencies. The following entries in the diary of Lady Paterson for the years 1831/2 vividly depict the life of Exeter's wealthier citizens.

CATHEDRAL YARD, EXETER

50

John Peltro sculp.

A FARM and VIEW near the River Ex in DEVONSHIRE.

London, Printed for ROBERT SAYER, Map, Chart & Printseller, No. 53, Fleet Street, as the Act directs, October 1st 1786.

1831

March

15th
Letter from James, wishing his father to become responsible for £700 which sum his uncle would advance upon that security, and James would be appointed to a Regement immediately. At first the General positively refused, as he lately advanced him so large a sum, but as James solemly promised to pay principal and interest in two years, his father has complied with his earnest entreaties.
17th
The General wrote a letter to my brother John and another to James, Satuday evening, and took them to the Post Office himself.
22nd
AGP, M.M.P., and Miss K. went to the theatre, Lady D'Urbans box, were well entertained, returned past 12 – I was amused reading Moore's life of Byron.

April

25th
A fine day till afterwards five, when it became gloomy and rained, for which I was sorry, as Alexander set off on the outside of the coach to Torquay and we particularly wished that he should see that beautiful place to advantage. His aunt kindly gave him £4 to defray his expenses to Plymouth and I hope he will have fine weather for his excursion. Exeter, which is thrown into great commotion, choosing a new Member, one who will vote for the Reform. The General accepted James bill for £700.
27th
A fine day. Mrs. King called for Margaret to go to the dancing school.
28th
A warm wet day, before breakfast was removed A.G.P. made his appearance. Not meeting with a conveyance to Plymouth he got into an Exeter coach, and arrived late last night at a quarter past eleven – too late to come home. He was very pleased with Torquay and the country he saw. No visitors.

May

5th
A letter from A.G.P. dated September, all well, he has received only two of my letters.
8th
Sunday, heard a very indifferent sermon. AGP sat at home all the morning in his room. He went to the Cathedral in the afternoon. Miss K. and M.M.P. walked there together. Mr. Short called and accompanied the General to Church. He is one of the radical Reformers.
17th
A beautiful warm morning delightful for the travellers, Jessy and Alexander left in the mail for London, felt excessively dull, not only at their departure but for other causes. A.G.P. I may never see again, my sister I hope I shall see return in good health and spirits.

June

8th
A fine day, but dust very disagreeable, wrote to Jessy and to James a long letter, but finding Margaret was going to put one into the Post Office for him, did not send mine. She drank tea and stayed till ten at Major Reads. I had just put on my old white satin slippers and made myself comfortable, when to my annoyance Mr. Hoopen stalked in, drank tea, and sat till near ten. I cannot imagine his motives for coming uninvited.
10th
A very heavy rain, the General sold the carriage for the small sum of £41. I am very glad we have got rid of it, as we make little use of it, and it was very provoking to pay the tax, and the stand for it likewise, and the Ostler etc.
16th
A fine day, but heavy shower in the evening. Wrote to John, began a letter to Jessy. Sir Henry Farrington and Mrs. Allen called, M.M.P. in town, she and the General went with Miss Kekewich to Miss Barings to tea, to meet some friends who had dined, amongst whom were Lady Duckworth, Major Read etc., and a Miss Anning, a great geologist, who has made some remarkable discoveries. Captain Halstead amused the company by his amazing dexterity and beautiful tricks with cards, they were ingenious and neatly done.
21st
A very beautiful morning. Sir H. Farrington's hay field looked a lively and rural scene, he had his military tent erected, and his large family amusing themselves. I wish it were a more permanent object. A letter from A.G.P. all well at Ramsgate. I wrote to James to say how much we were surprised and disappointed at his neither coming or writing. Miss E. Blunt, Miss F. Whittock, Mrs. Tothill called. For a wonder M.M.P. did not go out all day.

W. H. Bartlett. J. F. Lambert

THE SUBSCRIPTION ROOMS, & NEW LONDON INN, EXETER.

July.

22nd

A fine Day. M.M.P. called on Mrs. Worthy and others of our neighbours. Miss Chadwicke called and appeared more than usually dull. In the evening M.M.P. and Miss K. took a walk, she drank tea with us afterwards, we sat by the light of the moon, without candles, till ten, when our quiet party broke up. I sent Mary into town with a letter for James, a needless errand, as it will not reach him till Monday. I had a letter from the General who is quite reconciled to remain at Cheltenham, till James returns here.

26th

Excessively hot and dust beginning to fly. Mr. Farrington called to make an apology for not keeping an engagement he had made to accompany M.M.P. and her friend to the Theatre. For my part I think they are better without such a youthful beau, especially as they are to be in the same box with the Peamore family. The coach was ordered to be with them at 7, it was near 8 however before it came. They were among the latest and were much pleased with the performance of Kemble (in Juliet).

August

3rd

A warm dark dusty morning. James left us at one for Falmouth, I felt very dull, parting with him, I hope he will reach Gibralter in safety, and find himself happy with his new corps and brother officers. The Misses Whitlocke and Mrs. Tothill called whilst he was at luncheon, we did not therefore see them. I never deny myself, but in this instance we could not admit them. Miss Halstead called later and M.M.P. saw her. The General saw the Captain comfortably seated on the coach and in good spirits. Mrs. Kekewich is not so well again. M.M.P. walked with her friend in the Crescent after very heavy rain, the General went into town before tea, to put a letter into the Post Office for my brother John. Still very hot.

4th

A very sultry morning, with an unsettled appearance. M.M.P.'s little God daughter Adelaide Margaret Asment died on Sunday at 6 o'clock being quite well in the morning. She went in to see the baby in its coffin and gave the mother a sovereign.

18th

A cloudy day looking very like rain, but as I had proposed going to Pennsylvania we had a carriage and went there accordingly in a fly, rather a small conveyance for three with large bonnetts, large sleeves, full dresses, etc. The General sat very uncomfortable. Lady D'Urban and family at home. She received us very kindly, we extended our drive to Cowley Bridge. When we came home M.M.P. and I called upon Mrs. K. I thought she looked very ill. I had not seen her for three months. A very heavy rain in the afternoon.

24th

A gloomy looking day. The General went at eleven to attend the funeral of Colonel MacDonald the son of the celebrated Flora. He was ushered into the dining room, where a very beautiful breakfast was handsomely laid out, he received a satin hand band and scarf and gloves, and with three other gentlemen went in one of six mourning coaches and four to the Cathedral, where the service was performed by an Archdeacon. An elegant monument will be erected to his memory. His son in laws carriage with four spirited grey horses, added to the splendour of the funeral, which was a very expensive one and attracted a greater crowd than had ever been seen in the streets. M.M.P. went to see it pass. Miss K. and Mr. Gould Whitlock called, when she was out. They walked together in the rain to the park.

September

1st

A very heavy rain, it will do much good to the country. Miss K. called and practised for an hour, the General called upon Mr. Wolesly who with his family are come from the West Indies to reside in Heavitree, acquaintances of Lady D'Urban.

3rd

A fine morning. Invited Miss K. to accompany Margaret and I to call upon Miss Mitchell, for which purpose we hired a Barouche. Had a pleasant drive found the ladies at home. Rather a formal visit, as they had some visitors who gave themselves no trouble in conversation. The grounds about the cottage are laid out with taste. We were offered luncheon, which we saw was plentifully prepared, but we got neither the fruit nor flowers. We drove afterwards to town, the young ladies upon their return home agreed to take a walk and went accordingly back to Exeter. We had a letter from Alexander poor fellow. I rather expected he would have been able to make a flying visit here with his aunt, instead of which, he announces his departure for India, the ship to sail from Portsmouth on Monday. I wrote to that place to say farewell, a long farewell. God bless him.

6th

A fine morning. Mrs. Reid sent a brace of Partridge, she's very polite in these attentions.

Drawn from Nature & on Stone by Geo. Rowe 38 Paris Street. *Printed by P. Simonau.*

PENNSYLVANIA NEAR EXETER.

8th
The long talked of day is at length arrived. I trust our good King and Queen will be crowned without any annoyance, and all pass quietly. Heard that if we did not illuminate, our windows would be broken. The General and I in order to be prepared arrange 16 wax candles in the Drawing room. Mrs. and Miss Sanders called, M.M.P. went into Exeter with Miss K. The servants of course without considering the inconvenience to the family asked to go to see the illuminations. Had a letter from Alexander sent by the Pilot from the Roxborough Castle off the Isle of Wight. So poor fellow he is once more separated for a long period from his friends. We made a tollerable appearance with 16 candles in 2 windows, they were all extinguished before 11 and we retired to bed quietly. Heavy rain in the evening.

October

7th
A stormy wet day. Wrote a letter to Mrs. Jack, received one from the General. He is quite disappointed in his expectations, and intends leaving London on Sunday even. Nothing talked about but the Reform Bill.
21st
A very disagreeable wet day. We are still without our fire. M.M.P. called on Miss K. Mr. G. Teed called, a letter from James, he plainly tells us he has not the smallest prospect of paying the money he borrowed from his Uncle, therefore as the General has borrowed himself to pay it, if James did not, we must economise strictly to save out of his pay.

November

1st
I never sleep comfortably when any extraordinary event is going to take place, therefore expecting the man with his apparatus to sweep the kitchen chimney, I was awake at 3, and at 6 called the servants. Turned out a very wet day and no visitors. The General called on our neighbours.
4th
We hear the mob intend burning the effiges of the Bishop and five other gentlemen tomorrow being the anniversary of the Popish plot.
5th
A disagreeable wet day. Various rumours about burning and riot, but all went off quietly without disturbances. The domestic affairs not so tranquil, for the General locked the Garden gate at five and the servants were highly indignant at being made *prisoners*, although they were told that they would go out at the hall door.
13th
(Sunday) A tolerable fine day, though the wind was high. The General and M.M.P. twice at church, where was a collection for the church missionaries. Mrs. K. called. She is very seriously alarmed about the cholera as it is approaching and is a most appauling disease. Mr. Caird called on Jessy.

December

20th
A wet day, a fire in the drawing room as Miss K. came to practice and settle about going to hear Paganini, who is to perform 3 nights in Exon. Mrs. E. Casey and Miss Fartel from Torquay called.
22nd
A mild but damp morning, a letter from James, quite well, but no hint of trying to save any part of his pay. At 6 a coach came, which conveyed the General, M.M.P. and Miss K. to the concert where they were astonished and enraptured with the wonderful performance of Paganini. They returned after 11.
25th
(Sunday) and Xmas Day. The General not well, took some medicine which prevented his accompanying Jessy and M.M.P. to Church, the former alone in the afternoon. A remarkably fine day.
26th
. . . the General much better, many kind enquiries were made for him, as it was unusual circumstances to be absent from Church. Tormented all day with people coming for Xmas boxes.
31st
A very fine day. Mr. Caird called and Mrs. K., Miss Gifford called to accompany M.M.P. for a walk. I think it strange we have never heard of the arrival of the parcel I sent 10 days ago to Leyton, and also a fine large Turkey.

1832

January

18th
A very fine day. Breakfasted in bed. Jessy and M.M.P. still coughing a good deal. The latter tired of confinement at home so long, walked into Exeter. The shops there full of finery for the fancy Ball on

W.H. Bartlett. Le Petit.

GUILDHALL, FORE-STREET, EXETER.

TO THE MAYOR AND CORPORATION, THIS PLATE IS RESPECTFULLY DEDICATED, BY THE PUBLISHERS.

FISHER, SON, & C° LONDON 1829

Monday. The public much shocked with hearing that Colonel Breretor had committed suicide at Bristol. This gentleman was nephew to Colonel Coghlan, with whom we were well acquainted. In Exeter the recorder deprived himself of life, in a shocking manner. He was heir to the title and estate of Lord Rolle.

28th

A fine winter day. Martin Breconridge, Miss B. and Miss Worthy called Miss K. spent a long morning with M.M.P. The General received a leter from Baron Orrteda announcing that the King had been graciously pleased to nominate him a Knight Commander of the Military Hanovarian Gwelphic Order, which entitles him to be called Sir William, and poor I, my lady. I wrote to my brother.

February

10th

A still finer, sunshine, warm day, fortunately for our operations in the sweeping way, the Dining room and Kitchen chimnies were swept and both very foul. The man with his machine damaged the top of it, as he did before. I prefer the poor little boy, if we could be sure of no accident. Mr. Caird and his young son, Mrs. Campion and two daughters called. Had a complete day of cleaning and took our meals and sat all day in the Drawing room.

24th

A very beautiful sunny spring day. Many visits of congratulations.

25th

A letter from James, his conduct respecting money matters is very unfeeling, knowing how economically we live, to endeavour to pay the purchase of his Company. His father will be seriously incomoded by the request he has made.

May

10th

A cold dry day. Miss K. and Miss Teed called. M.M.P. went with Mr. Greenhill in her carriage to Pennsylvania, Lady D not at home. Heard of the change of Ministry, in consequence of the resignation of Lord Grey and his party. Sir William walked into town with the Halsteds and M.M.P. and heard Dr. Crooks introductory lecture. I cannot give my attention to any subject but the Reform Bill. Lighted the fire we had left off.

16th

Another dry day, a great cattle fair in Exeter, and a Conservative meeting to petition the King *against* Reform. I pity the poor King, who is idolised and eulogised one day, the next reviled and insulted, he will be more popular, as report says, now he has got back his late Ministers. Miss K. Whitlock and her brother John lately from India called. He is a leutenant in a Regiment of Native Cavalry. M.M.P. went out with Miss K. to see some wonderful horsemanship at the barracks and did not return until half past five.

June

28th

A very beautiful summer's day, but the heat overpowering. Put away the plate etc., and everything as usual arranged. I took a drive with Jessey, on the Topsham Road and home by Sandgate. Very tired after all my unusual exersions. Stopped at the Hotel to leave cards for the Douglas family. Heard Miss Tyrwhitt was in the house, and had been enquiring for her so we relunctantly left the carriage to shake hands with her. In the evening we were enjoying a prospect of a quietness till bed time, when we had two most unexpected visitors announced, Mr. and Mrs. Wilson. She an agreeable acquaintance we formed at Cheltenham, they had just left Xeres in Spain, where they reside, he being a wine merchant. They took tea with us. Miss MacDonald came to practice with M.M.P. who did not go out.

July

5th

Another hot dry day. After the breakfast was over had a sort of scene with Mary, who is very angry at my having given her warning, and finding another hired in her place. Told me she was going to be married, still supposing I would keep her a month longer, but that I am determined not to do, and she in consequance was richly impertinent. I shall be I hope more comfortable with strangers.

20th

A very fine day. Picking currants for a pudding which with some rasperries was excellent. M.M.P.'s cold better, Jessy complaining and I felt very poorly. Mrs. and Miss K. called. The former dreadfully alarmed about cholera, which has at length reached our hitherto healthy City, Exeter. Four new cases occurred this day, Mr. Caird called and is to send laudanum in case of emergency. I had a letter from my brother, this disease carries many off in his neighbourhood. He sets off to Scotland tomorrow.

The South side of the late South Gate

Exeter Pub^d. Septr. 1. 1834. at J. Gendall's, S^t. Peters Church Yard

G.F. Robson del[t]

W. Taylor sc.

N.W. VIEW OF

THE CITY OF EXETER.

To SIR THOMAS DYKE ACLAND BART. M.P. &c. &c. a patron of the Fine Arts and Literature, this plate is inscribed by the EDITOR

London. Published Dec. 1. 1827. by J. Britton, Burton Street.

Printed by Barnett & Son.

August

8th

A very beautiful morning for the races, to which I daresay many people will go in spite of the cholera.

17th

If possible a still more oppresive day, we all busy reading Mrs. Trollopes Domestic Scenes in America.

September

3rd

A fine day, Mr. & Miss Northmores called, he is endeavouring to get a seat in Parliament. M.M.P. called on Miss Chadwick yesterday and gave her a handsome pair of glove fasteners, as a parting remembrance, as that young lady is going home to Iceland. M.M.P. called on her friend Miss MacDonald, and Miss Baring, we were sitting at Tea, by Moonlight, when we were alarmed by a scream, a loud talking. Sir William went out and found Sir. H. Farrington standing beside his open carriage upset and his poor horse lying on its side. Miss Kekewich, Sir H. and his two daughters were unhurt, and certainly had a miraculous escape.

15th

A high wind, but fine morning. This day my brother John is to celebrate the anniversary of the birth of his eldest daughter, and his infant son to be christened, to whom Sir William is to be god father, together with Mr. Bissland and his sister as godmother. We drank their health in Claret. Miss Teed and her Brother George called, also Mr. Caird. M.M.P. accompanied Miss K. to Pennslvania in the Evening where they met an agreeable party, and were highly entertained with the private theatricals of Lady D'Urban, her 2 daughters, and governess. Their performance was excellent, and the characters remarkably well dressed. Parts of 'Douglas', 'The Provoked Husband', and 'Popping the Question,' were the entertainments. A fine night.

29th

A very fine morning, an agreeable breeze all day, which wafted many visitors to number 4. Miss MacDonald, Miss Dore, and Miss Kekewich came first, the latter accompanied M.M.P. to the Farringtons. They called to inquire for Miss Whittock, who is confined to the sofa, by a pain in her knee. Mrs. & Miss Gifford made a long visit, the former had not been in our house for upwards of a year, on account of severe and dangerous succession of illnesses. She is wonderfully recovered and her affectionate daughter is truly rejoiced and happy. They were scarcely departed when Mrs. K. called, she wished to ascertain, if our laundress had the the cholera, and I was sorry to say it was too true, as her son Mrs MacDonalds's servant, went to see his mother and had not returned. We of course would not have our linen sent home, neither can we employ the poor woman for some time. When we had given up all thoughts of any more visitors, Mrs. Kennedy came in. She is going to Cheltenham where she left her son and daughter the latter of whom is going to be married.

October

21st

A very fine day, Miss Pidsley, Miss Blunt, Miss Gifford called M.M.P. accompanied the latter and her Mama and (little dog in a basket) in a fly to Bishops Court, the Seat of the late unfortunate Lord Graves, where the furniture is to be sold, which is of a very poor description, the library is tolerably well supplied with Books. Jessy and M.M.P. walked afterwards into Exeter.

November

1st

A very stormy day. We lighted a fire in the drawing room, in expectation of Miss Kekewich and Mr. Dunbar, the latter an excellent performer on the violin, which he sent before him. Miss K. disappointed us, and did not come. We had some charming music, the tones of his Creniona very fine. He said he paid 150 guineas for it, and sold another for £50, he sang two songs very agreeably. Had a letter from James, all well.

5th

A stormy looking day, the wind high. Tormented with children and ragged Guy Fawks. Much shocked to hear of the death of the pretty little girl who had scarlet fever. Sir William went to the poor mother and gave her half a sovereign. She fears her husband* will soon leave her a widow as he is very ill. Some fatality appears to attend the MacDonald family. Another son is dead in India, killed in action. One coming home in bad health and the youngest not well in Ireland, the youngest daughter in a precarious state. Miss Teed called Jessy and M.M.P. walked into town. Lt. D'Urban called when they were out, in the event an invitation for M.M.P. from Lady D'Urban.

---

*Toll house keeper at Heavitree

December

3rd

A stormy day, occassional heavy showers, did not expect any visitors, but we had scarcely finished breakfast, when Mr. Atherby and three gentlemen were announced. They came to see the amount intended to be given by Sir William towards building a new church in Heavitree. He put his name for £10-10-0 a large sum for us, as we are only tenants for a short period and yet small if we expect to get a good seat. Sir William promises to give the same amount if or when the Church is finished.

25th

Christmas Day. A very dark, wet morning. I gave the servants a very pretty merino dress and lining. The sun shone beautifully all afternoon. Sir W. went to Church. Mr. Short called, Mrs. MacDonald called in a carriage for M.M.P. who dined with her and family and walked home in the evening. We passed a quiet day.

NORTHERNHAY - EXETER
From the New London Inn.

Certainly the Patersons and their friends enjoyed an urbane social life supported by all the modern delights of the time. The theatre which was near Bedford Circus and Southernhay, was a large building which after a fire in 1820 had been rebuilt. There is no longer a theatre in Southernhay, but the Northcott Theatre on the University campus provides a professional company, supplemented by performances at the Barnfield Theatre. Dancing and the theatre arts were just as important as the theatre. The City was well provided for in this respect. The Royal Subscription Rooms included in it a Ball Room of considerable size and elegance, and contained tea rooms and rooms sufficiently large and well equipped for all types of assemblies, concerts and exhibitions. The Devon and Exeter Hall was behind Fore Street and used for public meetings and concerts, but perhaps the most important of the places of amusement and education was the Athenaeum in Bedford Circus which was completed in 1835. It had lecture rooms, and was used by a variety of literary societies. These included the Exeter Literary Society founded in 1841, and the Scientific and Literary Institution established in 1844.

The Subscription Rooms, Devon and Exeter Hall and Athenaeum have gone, but the Devon and Exeter Institution still occupies its original premises in the Close. It was founded in 1813 and occupies what was once the town house of the Courtenays. Today, this privately run and supported institution is still thriving. There was of course the Public Select Library which had premises in the High Street and the Cathedral Library with 8,000 volumes in the Chapter House, where different types of books could be borrowed or read. There were specialist libraries - the medical libary at the Devon and Exeter Hospital and the Law Library at the Athenaeum. The opportunities for extending knowledge were quite considerable for most people of those times, although the present library in Exeter is incomparably better stocked than any that have preceded it.

The Cathedral and clergy held considerable sway in the nineteenth century, the building is still the most dominant in the City. Like most other places in Devon there was considerable ecclesiastical building work, the Bishops Palace was substantially rebuilt in 1845, new district churches arose in the suburbs. Some like that in St. Leonards (1833) and St. Michaels in Heavitree (1845) replaced earlier ones. It seems to have taken a dozen years to raise sufficient to complete the Heavitree church to which General Paterson contributed and in which a wall plaque commemorates the family. Others like St. Stephens in the High Street were modernised, and by 1850 there were 21 parish churches in the City. In addition to the Established Church, various chapels and other places of worship were built, amongst the earliest was the Unitarian Chapel of 1760 in South Street, and equally grand was the Mint completed in 1812 for the Wesleyans.

It was also a prolific time for school building. Some were of a sectarian

G. Townsend, del. Exeter
Pubd by H. Besley's Directory Office, South Street, Exeter

EXETER. (S.E.)

nature attached to chapels, like the one at the Mint, others like the various National Schools were freely available. About twenty schools of different sorts are listed in White's Directory, many of them supported by charitable trusts and offering a different emphasis in their approach to learning. Amongst these were some that had already been established for many years, including the Free Grammar School in the High Street established in Charles 1st reign. Those established in the first half of the Century included The Ladies Charity School in 1804 and Heles Boys' School which was housed in new buildings in new North Road in 1848/9.

As well as the normal educational establishments there were those for the deaf and dumb, and for the blind. The fore-runner of St. Lukes College, now incorporated into the University of Exeter, was to be found in the Close, where during the decade after 1840 about fifty young men and twenty young women were trained for the Church of England as school teachers. Necessarily the buildings and sites have changed and many of the schools that served the city have closed. The range of opportunity has been extended to a University and to specialist vocational training, but it has developed from what was a broad base established in early Victorian times in an effort to achieve excellence.

The City through a variety of trusts and the Guardians of the Poor endeavoured to provide for the paupers who were often aged and unable to fend for themselves. The Mayor and twelve Aldermen were those responsible together with forty others elected for life by the ratepayers of the four wards, for the administration of the charitable funds which in 1838 supplemented the poor rates. There was a workhouse off the Heavitree Road in the Eastern Suburbs for 550 paupers and in St. Thomas the Union Workhouse could shelter 450.

There were a good many almshouses which also helped to provide for the old and needy and many other charities were developed to cope with a variety of social needs. The Dispensary, in Queen Street, was established in 1818 and later moved to what is described as a "neat and substantial" building. The West of England Eye Infirmary, in Magdalen Street was founded in 1808, and now occupies a substantial stone and brick building opposite Wynards Hospital, which is a voluntary service centre, but was in the nineteenth century the home of twelve infirm poor people and a priest.

One institute, which had a peculiarly Victorian ring about its name, was The Devon and Exeter Female Penitentiary which when it was established in 1819 was lodged in a house fitted up to receive about fifty penitents. White states "its object is to afford an asylum to those unfortunate females who, having deviated from the paths of virtue, are desirous of being restored to their proper station in society, by religious instruction and the formation of moral and industrious habits. It has been the means of plucking many brands from the burning, and of solacing many parents by reclaiming their unhappy

STEPCOTE HILL, EXETER

Stepcot Hill near Westgate

Exeter Pub.d Sep.r 1 18.. J. Gendall's St. Peter's Church Yard

Isaac Bird del. C. Hullmandel Lithog.

BROAD GATE . EXETER .

Pub. by John Treadwin, 217 High St. Exeter, Aug 15 1822

daughters from the lowest haunts of vice and degradation. It is supported by subscriptions and donations." Corresponding to this for men there was the Devon and Exeter Refuge for the instruction and employment of Discharged prisoners which in 1835 came to Sidwell Street. There are of course echoes of these institutions to be found in our own attempts to help the deprived, needy and less able members of society, which often supplement government or local authority provision.

To modernise the City and make it clean and efficient it became necessary to remove the street markets, which had flourished for centuries amidst smells, noisiness and rowdiness, and not a little good humour. In 1835/6 Western Market in Fore Street was built and later the Eastern Market in Queen Street, design by George Dymond, was completed. St. Georges Hall in Fore Street is the modern successor to these whilst Dymond's Market in Queen Street is used for small shops. The cattle, sheep, horses and other beasts were moved to Exe Island, and now the weekly market is held at Marsh Barton, conveniently close to the main road serving a modern industrial estate.

In 1817 the first gas lit streets of the City flickered into being, and the Gas Works on Exe Island gradually supplied all Exeter and its suburbs. It was not until 1833 that the polluted supplies of water from ancient acqueducts and wells were replaced by water pumped from the Exe to a reservoir, before being distributed through iron pipes throughout the City. Some improvements were forced upon the City, particularly in the case of electoral reform and the management of the Borough.

The Commissioners on Municipal Corporations visited Exeter in 1834 and found the City as well run as most in the country, although they were critical of the £100,000 debt incurred on running the Canal. In 1825 the Corporation employed Mr. James Green to deepen the canal and extend it to Turf. Improvements to the quay at Exeter in 1830 provided a ship basin where occasional steam packets called but more frequently it was used by larger sailing vessels. This expenditure was not well reviewed by the Commissioners nor was the muddled way in which the various trusts, managed by the Corporation were handled. There was a total of £17,000 owed to some of them as a result, although fifteen years later much property which had been held in trust had been restored. On the adoption of the Commissioners recommendations following the Municipal Reform Act of 1835, new government was introduced to the City, headed by a mayor, twelve aldermen and thirty-six councillors.

Before 1800 the City was beginning to shrug off the less pleasant aspects of its medieval and Elizabethan past and look to the future. To improve the environment became the passion of those with wealth and to provide for the less fortunate a duty. By 1850 there were many new buildings and public open spaces. Queen Street was largely built in 1835 and is still an attractive part of the centre, the Iron Bridge of the same year is an outstanding piece of engineering as are the warehouses down on the Quay. Bury Meadow is now a mature open garden and this was first opened to the public in 1846. Northernhay had always been a promenade and was restored after a period of neglect, and Southernhay was also laid out.

For the person who lived in Exeter in the first half of the nineteenth century there were a variety of walks and picturesque scenery with both new and old buildings of considerable interest to be seen as they strolled along. To the Victorian the many handsome villas and rows of genteel houses with tasteful gardens, shrubberies and woody lawn were the true statement of success and urban harmony.

Today the scale of life has enlarged still further, but it is the ancient buildings, parks and engineering that do most to create the spaciousness and prosperous character of Exeter. The Ancient Guildhall in High Street stands amongst a variety of buildings left from other ages and points to the continuity as well as its long history. Amazingly after the devastation of war years and the amount of building in the past thirty years, it still provides a civilized environment, however changed. Like Plymouth much of the centre was rebuilt following war damage, and here it was the use of brick that predominated in the bland fashion of the 1950s, with not a lot of elegance but quite considerable convenience. Although buses still pass through the centre, the cars have gone and shoppers can wonder at will, although like many towns much of the quality of the old centre has been changed by road widening, car parks and the predominance of the motor car in general.

Over three-quarters of those employed in the City are engaged in service industries, looking after shops, working in offices, organising but not manufacturing. At the Quay the vessels no longer sail with goods to other coastal ports, and the basin and one of the tall Heavitree Stone warehouses that stand by it are occupied by the Maritime Museum. It is a pleasant place to be but no longer one where a torrent of commerce sweeps other things aside.

There are no longer local private banks to promote commerce, just the national ones, although there are still the multitude of Insurance Companies and tradesmen. New walks along the River, playing fields and a parks department intent on planting every scrap of spare space in the town centre have helped to keep the feeling of spaciousness, and quality. It is a pity that the Lucombe oak, a hybrid species introduced to Exeter in 1792 by a City market gardener is not being replanted to ensure that this little bit of sylvan history is not lost forever.

W. Harvey, del. From a sketch by J. Thorne. T. A. Prior, sc.

EXETER.

5. Tour of Dartmoor

by the Reverend John Swete

The following pages will contain the result of two excursions to the Forest of Dartmoor. The first taken during the month of August 1795 in the company of my friend and relation the Reverend Henry Beeke, the latter during the August of the present year, (1797) to which I was induced by the personal solicitation of the Honorable Mr. Justice Buller.

On Sunday 20th August at half past four in the evening I quitted Oxton, passing over Haldown by Penwill to Doddiscombsleigh. In my descent of a long hill to this place I had a very picturesque view of the Church and village, seated on a knoll, and surrounded by verdant pastures.

Bridford bridge lying at a distance of a mile and a half from hence soon came in view. From a wild eminence down whose steep northern declivity I passed it was a striking object, nor was the landscape that spread itself out in farms, orchards, and inclosures, on the slope of a hill across the glen at the foot of the common, devoid of rural and picturesque traits.

Riding through the hamlet of Lee Cross, I came to the Bridge which lay over the Teign. Having crossed a mill leat, at the commencement of a hill I had a fine view of the Wear which diverted this Water stream from the Rivers bed. The waters were low, and in consequence the dam across the channel appeared as a long ledge of huge rounded stones, piled irregularly one on another. The ascent, confined within a deep and narrow lane became steep.

The summit of the hill introduced me to a track of country, which Nature had reclaimed from the hand of man. The vestige of enclosures continued, but the produce of the land was furze and rushes. Towering in the midst of these, having left the vast mass of Hell Torr behind I came near the Rock of Blackstone.

The evening was now closing in, and a thick drizzling rain hastened on the night which overtook me a short while before I entered the town of Moreton Hampstead. At the Inn I found all those comforts which a traveller, not fastidious, would desire from wholesome fare, neatness and civility.

The town of Moreton, in general mean and dirty, has nothing of consequence annexed to it, but its Church. This is seated on an eminence at the north east end, and exhibits itself in an exceedingly picturesque manner, when viewed from a piece of water at some distance up a northern glen.

The water has been pounded for the use of a brown paper Manufactory which is carried on lower down the valley. At that part of it also, which skirts the base of the eminence on which the Church stands, the Parsonage House is situated. It is a large and rather handsome pile, but lying very low, in a narrow defile, among high hills, it is necessarily subject to damps. The living however is rich enough to compensate this inconvenience of its Rectory, in the disposal of Lord Courtenay, and under the incumbency of my neighbour Mr. Clack who is also rector of Kenn. With his eldest son who has just taken orders, and who, serving the cure, resides in the Parsonage House, I breakfasted the next morning, and as there were parts of the Teign at Fingle bridge I had not seen he was so good to accompany me hither.

We were now riding on an emminence, from whence we had a view of the Country around Exeter beautifully tinted with a cast of blue. Passing from hence by Cranbrook Farm, above which towards the west rose high the Castle or Entrenchment, we began our descent to the River Teign.

The countryside that fringes the high open moorland offers some of the most pleasant landscape in the county. It is often well wooded broken country with many vantage points and pleasant views. In 1800 much of the hillsides above the Teign Valley and close to Doddiscombsleigh were unenclosed and probably used for rough grazing, but since then the hillside plantations that now add such variations and colour to the scene have been planted and the open land enclosed as pastures. It is estimated that about 30,000 acres of common land around the edges of Dartmoor were enclosed between 1820 and 1850. Doddiscombsleigh is a small village with houses straggling along a road on a ridge with views over nearby valley lands. The parish had 375 people in 1850, who supported a clothing club and lending library. St. Michaels is a pleasant fifteenth-century church, the social focal point of the village down the ages.

MORETON CHURCH.

Lithotint from Nature by W. Spreat.
C. Hullmandel's Patent.

The River Teign runs close to Leigh Cross which has probably changed even less than Doddiscombsleigh. There are no more than two or three houses nearby including a neat thatch and cob farm house. A short step from this picturesque spot is Bridford Bridge, and the route which Swete took towards Hell Torr.

The poorer land of Dartmoor, exposed and difficult to farm, has probably been affected less than any in the County by development. Hell Torr and the impressive slab of Blackingstone Rock are unchanging features in places where the harsh winds and poor soils have never helped the farmer. Moretonhampstead has always depended for its prosperity on farming, and several cattle fairs were regularly held there. In 1827 the Lord of the Manor built a new Market House and Shambles for the farming community. A bleak position did not stop a lively social life with ten inns and several non conformist chapels, of which three were built between 1817 and 1824. It was certainly no more isolated than other small towns in Devon, with adequate roads to Exeter and across the Moor to Tavistock.

The town has much the same atmosphere today and the granite church of St. Andrews perched on a steep hill on the east side of the town is impressive from the Exeter Road some way away. The paper mill has long since gone. There is nothing mean or squalid about the town today, and if it lacked grandeur it has never lacked much else.

Cranbrook Castle is an ancient fortification south of, and above the River Teign on a heathy high spur bordering coniferous plantations, with wide views over the countryside.

The declivity was long and steep. Deep delving through coppice and woods, which precluded every view beyond themselves, excepting it were now and then, at the flexures of the road which being more open permitted me to enjoy fine retrospective views of prominent and receeding hills raising their high crests to the skies, alternately craggy and wooded, through which, the rapid River rolled down its foamy waters.

On reaching the bottom we crossed a leat that ran to a Grist Mill on the right, and following the road to the left we came to the bridge.

The view indeed above the bridge is of a grander nature than that below. The mountainous precipices are more abrupt and elevated, and as they rise over the arches in barren majesty impress on the mind of the beholder conceptions of sublimity, blended with others of the wildest desolation. It is succeeded by another of a softer cast, the interchange from rough creast to woods and thickets is most delightful. Perhaps there are no parts of this River, that are so admirably beautiful and Romantic, as those in the vicinity of Fingle Bridge.

At a mile or so above, at the commencement of Whiddon Park the Hills begin to be more than usually elevated, and to form themselves into these stupendous screens and vast barriers against which the waters of the boisterous Teign through a succession of ages have been in vain. A continuance of these magnificent features may be marked till the approach of the river to Clifford bridge, loosing however, by insensible gradations their rugged aspect which by the accession of Woods on both sides, becomes mellower and more soft.

Fingle bridge is situated in the very midst of this magnificent scenery whose elevated hills, rounded on their summits, are frequently divided from each other, by narrow glens.

Mr. Clack returning to Moreton, I proceeded onward to Drewesteignton. The church and tower were handsome in their Architecture, and materials being large, of the Gothic cast, and composed of granite.

The Parsonage house being contiguous, with the Rector Doctor Roberts, I sat half and hour. From the building itself, surrounded by offices and outhouses there is no prospect but from a garden green on its eastern aspect. The view opening over the country I had passed through, had not only extent but magnificence.

The eye was indeed unable to penetrate into the depths between the mountains through which the River Teign rolled its waters, and the rich scenery of woods that decorated their sides was lost to it. The whole was wild and grand, and though not in a state of culture, was yet admirably adapted to the maintenance of large flocks of sheep, a

J. Strutt, Del.

Duncan, Sculp.

TEIGN HEAD IN DARTMOOR.

Published by W. J. Strutt & Son, Exeter & Teignmouth.

Printed by Fisher, London.

moreling breed, which when fattened in richer pastures, which the Parish also can well supply, produce admirable mutton, which for flavour, will yield to none in the Kingdom.

On our descending a hill towards the bottom of a common, I immediately recognised a track which in a former visit to this Parish conducted me to the enormous logan stone that was situated on a ledge of rock in the bed of the Teign.

Having past the hamlet of Sandy Park, which had before led me to the Cromlech, we came to Rushford, where had formerly been a house of some consequence and a chapel that had been demolished by its last proprietor Major Hoare. Instead of the old mansion there is now a neat farmhouse. Rushford Bridge over the River Teign soon after presented itself, which with a mill that I had just before passed had received its appelation from the Mansion of Rushford. From a meadow above the bridge the scene was picturesque, but it had lost its wild association of steep hills, rough rocks, and overhanging wood. It was no longer a rapid foaming clamourous River, but flowing in an even tenor, and with a motion scarce perceptible, it glided through the level pastures and reflected in its lucid bosom every object that impended over its banks.

I proceeded on my way to the town of Chagford, which lay about half a mile distant. The situation of the town, on a hill sloping from the south is dry and salubrious, nor is its appearance, as seen from Rushford bridge devoid of some traits of the picturesque. The mountainous hill at its back is indeed a singularly attractive object, whether it is to be considered as to its vast bulk, or as to its figure, which is that of a massive cone, terminating in three rocky summits, the middlemost of which is most elevated. All the buildings in the place I found mean and irregular, exclusive of the Parsonage House, which lies somewhat to the South East of the Church.

This edifice is large and of Gothic Architecture is well seated, and has within it a monument with a concise and simple inscription to the memory of Sir John Whyddon, one of the justices of the Kings Bench in the reign of Queen Mary. The place is one of four stannery towns of the County, and the Rectory is possessed of by the Reverend John Hayter, whose uncle was Bishop of London, and in whose family, the patronage of the living has continued from the year 1742.

Having at a pothouse taken a mutton chop and fed my horses, soon after four I quitted the town by an outlet to the North west. But this road leading direct to Gidleigh, and as the farm of Sir Francis Buller in the midst of Dartmoor was the object I was in quest of, at the end of the street I turned more to the west. From the ford of a stream,

LEFT: BLACKINGSTONE ROCK

the road began in ascent, which ended not till I had attained one of the Heights of the Forest.

After I had ridden near two miles at a cross lane I was met by a carrier with several horses laden with lime. Conversing with him on the subject as we moved up the hill together, I found that he had been to the neighbourhood of Ashburton for his manure, a distance of 12 miles, and for which he set out before day break. Surprised at this account as I well know, that there were calcarious rocks nearer, both at South Tawton and Drewesteignton, I yet further interrogated him, as to the reason, why he had gone to a much greater distance, for a commodity than there was any apparent cause for. His answer was, that though South Tawton was but 7 miles, and Drewesteignton four, yet as these kilns were situated so far inland there was frequently a deficiency of Culm, and that the assurance of being always able to procure lime at the Ashburton kiln and that without detention, which was almost always the case at the other places, more than compensated for the greater remoteness and labour.

The River Teign was of particular interest to Swete, who followed it on other occasions observing the various Mills and memorable pastoral scenes about it. Whatever the changes a walk from Steps Bridge near Dunsford on past Clifford Bridge to Fingle Bridge at Drewsteignton and then, on to Chagford, can be an exhilarating and rewarding as any in the County. A convenient car park at Steps Bridge, and the obtrusive but welcome cafe at Fingle Bridge, followed by a collection of good pubs at Chagford underpin a pleasant day's walk. At first the oak, ash, sycamore and alder grow commonly beside the path with plenty of silver birch to lighten the scene. From Clifford's bridge the path passes by a plantation of conifers which in turn gives way to oak, ash and other hard woods from Fingle Bridge to Chagford. New conifer plantations have been planted, or have replaced broadleaved woodland but the towering hills, and tumbling waters of the Teign and an abundant wildlife have changed little. Cliffords Bridge has been rebuilt and the ancient precarious stepping stones at Rushford Mill have probably worn a little more so that the use of the nearby road bridge is safer.

Dunsford, whose church of St. Mary houses the impressive monuments to the Fulfords, the Lords of the Manor in the early nineteenth century, and who still live at Great Fulford House, was built on a ridge, with thatch and

FULFORD HOUSE, DREWSTEIGNTON

Engrav'd by W. Angus from a drawing by H. Cornish, Esq.[r] for the Beauties of England & Wales.

GREAT FULFORD HOUSE.

The Seat of Baldwin Fulford Esq.[r]

Devonshire.

London Published by Vernor & Hood Poultry May 1 1804

white walled cottages beside it. These cottages, bulging where bread ovens were placed by large chimney stacks, must be almost as old as the church itself. The chancel of the church was built in 1841 but it is mostly an ancient granite building with medieval roof beams.

Drewsteignton's Church, St. Peter seems even more impressive than that at Dunsford, towering a little beyond the eastern edge of a neat little square, surrounded by thatched cottages, with the added charm of the Drewe Arms and its hitching post. Besides the compact village about the square there are several excellent gentlemen's houses around. On clear days the switchback countryside stretches away for miles, with trees and folds in the ground hiding small farms and giving a glimpse of others. The Drewsteignton Quarries provide limestone for roads and general building purposes, and around 1850 a valuable tin and copper lode was discovered at Drascombe farm in the parish which also yielded some silver. The mining ended many years ago although some traces of the working are still there. Castle Drogo built in the 1920s stands high on a hill spur overlooking the Teign Valley about a mile west of the village, and is open to the public and worth a visit. The logan stone which once stood in the bed of the Teign about a mile south of Shilston farm is no longer to be found.

Chagford is a small, neat town on the eastern side of the Teign Valley which can be seen from several miles away if approached from the Cranbrook Castle direction. Possibly the landscape of wide and wooded hill slopes help reduce the effect of the rather mundane modern houses on its edge. It was a market town and had four corn mills and a woollen industry which was already in decline when the factory closed in 1848. Three chapels were built in the early part of the century for the Wesleyans, Baptists and Bible Christians, and a new Rectory House was built for the parson of St. Michael's. The Church, built of granite, is 15th Century and although changed inside over the years, including the insertion of a modern rood-screen, has an enduring toughness, and dominance.

The square and roads leading from it are congested and busy with cars parked wherever space allows, and pedestrians struggling with arms full of shopping. The Three Crowns hotel is a notable early sixteenth century property built of granite and once the home of the Whiddon family. There are several other equally attractive inns close to the centre, and the Market House built there in 1862 replaced an earlier one.

A Logan Stone near Drew. Steignton, Devon
W & G Cooke sculp. 1805

BOWERMAN'S NOSE _ *Dartmoor.*

I now had reached the extent of the inclosed country, and passing through Tawton gate entered on the moor. As I had a glimpse of the Moreton turnpike road at a considerable distance, I was now at a loss whither to bend my steps. On my approach to the turnpike, I found myself surrounded by inumerable rabbits, and recognising a house or two by the wayside, discovered that I was at Mead's Warren. To it there was no fence but a few stones piled on one another, and ranged in a certain line, evidently serving to ascertain its limits than to preclude the rabbits from roving: indeed on the dry hill beyond this barrier or boundery they appeared to me as numerous, as they were within the restricted line, whose inclosed area, consisted in a great measure of an old stream works, lying in a hollow, and bearing a strong resemblance to the crater of an exhausted volcano. Nothing could be more wild and rugged than this spot.

Passing on from Meads Warren for a mile or two the prospect was of the most dreary nature, the horizontal line on every quarter was formed by the hills and Torrs of Dartmoor – a wide waste where the eye found not a point to rest on.

Post bridge lies about 2 miles from the Warren in the road to Tavistock and just before I approached it, I skirted two farms, situated to the right and left of the way, and called Higher and Lower Merrypit. The grass had not yet been mowed, and the oats were perfectly green.

The old bridge was in pretty good repair before the new one was erected a little above it. Tis impossible to form a conception of a structure more simple than this, or better adapted to the situation. It at present consisted of but three stones in length which placed imposts on pieces of the same kind, extended from one side of the water to the other. Whatever stones had been raised at the ends, so as to facilitate the ascent had been removed, having assisted perhaps in the construction of the New Bridge.

This bridge, that at Dartmeet, on the same river the East Dart, with a great many others, of like structure, on Blackabrook, West Dart, Cherry brook and Swincombe Rivers, were the only bridges on the Moor before the formation of the turnpike roads. On these travellers on foot, and on horseback were known to pass, and the report of the country is that by the same means carriages have crossed the rivers.

On my approach to the Old Post bridge I met with one of the miners who worked at Mead Warren. On questioning him as to the present state of the mine and its produce, he told me that it would not be said to be in a flourishing condition, for though the one was considered good, yet the lodes were neither large, nor easy to be worked, and that till late very little tin had been sent to the smelting house.

Pursuing my ride again, all was wild, and unviolated Nature. I surveyed a vast tract of verdant ground, free from rocky protuberancies, that fell in declivities towards the banks of the East Dart, from the high northern karn of Long-be-tor, but that was as fine a farm as any on the Moor might here be found, and that with reasonable expectations of a good success as had resulted from any other.

The New Take of Bellever which I soon after skirted, belonging to the Reverend John Templer, and that of Smith's lying westward of it, though consisting each of them of many hundred acres, can never return an interest adequate to the sums that have been expended by the Proprietors in the erection of these dry walls of granite. The ground within them remains in the status quo it was in, before it was inclosed, and the sole advantage that can accrue from it is a restrictive to a determinate number of cattle and their greater security.

I had left Bellever Torr on my left, and a range of several more elevated ones on the right consisting of Be yon torr, Waydown torr, South be torr, Long be Torr, and soon after passed under Crockern Torr. Crockern Torr lies lower than any other torr in the neighbourhood, and is much less compact. The pile instead of being one congregated mass, seems as if it had been shattered by some convulsion. Its parts consisting of huge blocks of granite lie spread around in every direction.

On my former visit to the Moor, I took this karn in my ride to Wistmans woods, which lies about a mile further northwoods, and from the consideration that on this torr the Stannery Parliaments had been held from a very remote age. In later times no business has been done on this spot.

Prince Hall, lay just before me as it were, and but a short distance if I had crossed the Moor, yet as it had grown late and I had some reason to be apprehensive of bog I kept on the Turnpike road till it found a junction with the Ashburton one near Two Bridges, and then turning left, in less than a mile I reached Prince Hall.

On alighting in the Court, I met with a sore disappointment, in finding from a servant that in consequence of a sudden illness Sir Francis Buller had been detained at his seat of Lupton. The reception however which I met with from the Reverend Mr. Yarde, his relation and constant companion in all his visits to Prince Hall reconciled me in part to the absense of the Judge.

The next morning under Mr. Yarde's escort, I mounted my horse, having proposed as objects of our ride, a waterfall formed by the

CROCKERN TOR _ *Dartmoor.*

stream that had lately been conducted to the Dock Yard, Mr. Tyrwhitts New Building and plantations, and the new discovered tin mine.

Having returned to the Moreton road, we descended the hill to two bridges. At this place there are two rivers, which are the West Dart, and the Cowsick, where with the most impetuous rapidity it rushes down a steep and confined channel. On the distant ground rises a small fir plantation, which has been attempted with some little success by the proprietor of the farm through which the Cowsick runs. This is called Bear down, and belongs to Mr. Bray, a gentleman resident at Tavistock.

On the public road a little Inn had been a few years ago erected by Sir Francis Buller for the accommodation of the travellers on the Moor. The spot was most judiciously selected, being nearly at the junction of several roads proceeding from Plymouth, Tavistock, Ashburton and Moreton Hampstead, and at a central stage as it were from them all.

Without stopping longer at present at "two Bridges" I shall proceed onwards to the Dock Leat. Taking the road to Plymouth we passed round the side of a hill, which soon after by a gentle descent brought us to Blackabrook. This was a rapid stream with the same character of wildness and obstruction in its course by means of large stones of granite, as all the moor rivers have in common. Its channel here was deep between quick sloping hills, at but a little distance however above, these declivities lost themselves in the more expanding valley, and from thence was descried the commencement of the Dock leat.

We now made our way towards Mr. Tyrwhitts plantation, the wall of which we saw rising the hill before us. But in our progress we met with very boggy ground, and the little morassess lay so close together that we found no small difficulty to advance with security.

We now gained the summit of the hill, and had reached some labourers who were working on the wall that was to surround the grounds. On questioning one of them I found that he had taken the wall at six pence per land yard, that he was not only to build it, but collect the materials, which by the efforts of oxen and a slide he procured from the contiguous parts of the Moor.

Whether that these were more perservering than horses or that they had been more accostomed to the morasses it was a confirmed fact, he told me, that they would through their labour with greater facility and with much less expense complete their work. The walls, as they are commonly raised consist of granite blocks, as large as human strength can manage with the aid of a lever which are lain one on another according to their natural forms, whether they have angles or not, and in general adjusted with considerable skill. This is termed dry stone wall, that is without cement, and is common to all wild countries, where there are stones ready at hand. Protected by such a nurse the plantations, have doubtless a fairer chance for a prolongation of existence if not stature.

Having encountered the perils of another bog, as we quitted Mr. Tyrwhitts premises we ascended a short hill to a shaft where we saw two men at work with a windlass. The lode which they were pursuing had been discovered about 3 years, by mere accident, in cutting the channel for the Dock Leat, and had turned out so productive, as to induce the Proprietors, Mr. Grey and others, to erect a smelting house and stamping mills, in the bottom beneath on the banks of a small stream, which emptied itself into Blackabrook.

This mine was called Batchelors Hall, employed 16 men, and with those of the Warren and Fox tor Meers, comprised the whole of what were now worked in Dartmoor.

We had wiled away so many hours in this our ramble, that I had no opportunity of inspecting the Smelting House. It was four oclock, and we were yet at a distance from Prince Hall.

Leaving these buildings therefore a little on the right, we descended yet further to the River Blackabrook, which on account of the vast masses of rounded granite in its channel we had some difficulty in fording. From thence we made our way, with what speed we could over a morassy track to Two Bridges, where we found the Landlord and others busily engaged in the erection of booths, and standings for a fair which was to be held there on the morrow. These, having past through, we soon finished our excursion, and having joined Mr. Crook sat down to our dinner with appetites not a little whetted by the keen action of the mountain air.

On this day was the anniversary of the Fair which had been this time two years instituted by the Judge. It was rather a singular circumstance that by mere accident I should have been present at both. At this latter fair, the appearance of sheep and cattle was pretty nearly the same, as on the former. The only difference arose from a number of Scottish black cattle which Mr. Crook, had introduced on the Moor, and which having in a great measure fattened during the summer on Smiths new take, which he rented off the Judge at £40 per annum, he sold at the rate of £7 or £8 per head. Sir F. Buller however had some years before procured a few of this breed from Scotland, having inferred with his wonted acumen, that an animal which had been bred on the bleak downs in North Britain would easily assimilate with a pasturage of the same nature elsewhere.

POSTBRIDGE AND NEW BRIDGE

In our way through Two bridges, between six and seven, we found the Fair at its height in point of revelry and pastime. The women however not yet emboldened by use, had in a great measure withdrawn, and the amusements of the men seemed to be confined to wrestling and drinking.

The open moorland and its ancient farms have probably changed relatively little. The Warren House Inn stands on the side of the B3212, which was once the toll road, and looks across a bleak valley. The traces of disused mines are witnessed by the broken ground, as it was 180 years ago.

At Post Bridge the National Park have a neat car park and information centre surrounded by fine mature beech trees. There are a number of relatively new houses in the vicinity but nothing to spoil the ancient simplicity of the post bridge and toll road bridge that replaced it.

Without doubt the coniferous plantations have changed the face of the Moor, although most of the tors and surrounding wild landscape is unaltered. At two bridges, the hotel has got larger since it was built by Sir Francis Buller and together with its bridge has been skirted by the present road. Close by on the Tavistock Road is Bear Down Farm with its plantation of conifers beyond. Wistmans wood unchanged, on the western bank of the Dart, is about a mile north of Two Bridges and is a good excursion from it. Not far along the road is the Blackabrook and Dock Leat not too distant from Dartmoor Prison. The prison was built in 1808/9 as a result of Sir Thomas Tyrwhitt persuading the Government it was a good place for prisoners of war, and stands sombrely in a bleak landscape.

Sir Francis Buller purchased Prince Hall estate from Mr. Gullet, and like Sir Thomas Tyrwhitt improved the area. Occasionally Sir Francis lived at Prince Hall which is a substantial two storey Georgian building found at the end of an impressive drive lined by beech trees. The house is privately owned and off the public road, and enjoys the seclusion and shelter of mature trees around it, as well as the West Dart below and to the south of it. The optimistic enclosure and planting seem to have succeeded, and the number of black cattle grazing on the Moor indicate the continuing success and value of Scottish breeds.

BRENTOR

Engrav'd by J. Storer from a drawing by S. Prout. *for the Beauties of England and Wales.*

BREN-TOR, AND CHURCH,
Devonshire.

London, Publish'd by Vernor & Hood, Poultry, Nov. 1, 1804.

Passing Cators farm, the evening mist debarred all afterview, and night preceeded us to Tavistoke.

The Abbey drew me early from my bed the next morning, the fine remains of this antique edifice could not fail of causing reiteration of the delight I had formerly felt in viewing them, and for two hours I continued my researches in defiance of drizzling rain, though the result of them was attended by little novelty.

The environs of the town, now cleared by the sun of the mist that had enveloped it, I found to be extremely picturesque. Our way at first led us by the banks of the Tavy, which offered to our view several very pleasing traits, and from the height, which were soon after gained, we had the command of a most rich and beautiful valley through which the River winded its foamy streams. Where the town exhibited itself finely in the midst of the surrounding hills, and chiefly on its western part where the fretted turrets of the Abbey rising above the rest arrested the eye by their singular elegant appearance.

From the pleasing and the Picturesque however the scene was soon shifted to that of a more rude and wild nature. On Merrivile Down we had a view of a singular Torr on the right called Vixen, and beyond, the Downs of Sampford Spiney and Walkampton. From this by an unpleasant descent we came to Merrivile Bridge and hamlet. The River Walkham here tumbles over as rocky a channel as can be imagined, forming throughout the whole course a succession of waterfalls.

At Pily brook to which we soon after came, where its stream crossed the turnpike road, I remarked with admiration one of the most excellent Paves I had ever seen composed of flat granite stones of massive bulk, contiguous to which was Randall's stone and those considerable stream works, denominated from it.

By previous appointment, which the Judge had yesterday taken the trouble of making for us, we were here met by an old man of the name of Cator, whose cot I observed by the wayside, as we passed from Prince Hall to Tavistoke.

This person having resided long on the moor, and being well acquainted with the whole of it, we had engaged as our liceroni, to point out to us what was remarkable on the Forest. To our great disappointment it happened that for the last hour the fog had been returning, and the misty vapours now so thickly enveloped the Tors on every quarter as to shroud them from our view. These the old man told us were his only land marks, and without they were visible, so that he might be able to discern their several bearings to each other, he would not dare to hazard our safety, by making an attempt to conduct us across the trackless and dangerous waste to Okehampton.

We gave up the scheme and proceeded onwards with Old Cator to his cottage. He told us that he was 77 years old, that he had a large family of children, and grandchildren, but that he was well able to maintain himself by his own labour without assistance.

> "I have placed out two of my sons in little farms like my own and at but little distance from it, and I have grandchildren at home that look to me for their supplies, and they shall have them. For, thank God though I am near four score, I am yet strong and heart whole, and when I set about it with spirit, I can earn four or five shillings a day cutting turf. Few people have worked harder than I have done in my day. When I first undertook to look after the roads on Dartmoor I took a good deal of them to make by the job, and as I found that a great deal of time was lost by going for shelter to some house at many miles distance, and returning again in the morning, during the summer months, wrapt up in a rugg and with a wisp of straw under my head I have lain myself down to sleep under a dry bank, and have always slept as sound as a top."
>
> "The winter," continued the old man "at length set in, and as no constitution can weather that, at least on the Forest, I thought of raising a sort of a house or shed, which might give me shelter. Accordingly I got a grant of a new take here (we were now arrived at his cottage, just by the head of Blackabrook) and by degrees I worked up with my own hands, some walls, which I cover with turf and long grass, and this little hovel was by additions which I have since made to it grown to what you now see, here I have lived for the last seventeen years."

I found the interior of the cottage to correspond in every respect with the outward appearance. The door entered into a portion appropriated to the winter reception of cattle belonging to the farm, from thence I passed directly into the kitchen, which was lighted by a sort of window, at the farther end was a large chimney in which blazed a cheerful peat fire, of which fuel as it rose at the indoor they did not seem to be sparing. Near the entrance I observed a ladder which I concluded, must lead to the bed chambers. Up this I ran, and found it to be so, in the singular number, for it consisted but one. About 20 feet in length and half that space in breadth, in which as close to each other as those in the long chamber of the College of Eton, there were ranged five beds in which without the interposition of screens or curtaining, the Old Man, his son, and others, amounting to four men, and five

T. Allom. S. Fisher.

TAVISTOCK, FROM THE LAUNCESTON ROAD.

women, every night took their rest. How patriarchal and in the ancient style of doing things.

Dartmoor was in an early period overun with wood, I shall describe with more particular notice of Wistmans Wood which I have already visited. From Crockern Torr it lies directly North at near a mile distance, and is situated on the slope of a hill rapidly falling to the West Dart, which hurries down a rugged channel immediately beneath it. Exclusive of the wood being found in the midst of Dartmoor the trees themselves, in their external appearance, indicating extreme age, are a most singular curiosity.

What their age may be, no records, or tradition are at hand to ascertain, their knarled branches, hastening visibly to decay, and the parasitical excrescence, moss, with which many of the limbs are enveloped, even to the thickness of a foot, are manifest testimonials of their ancient birth. Perhaps they may have claim to an origin, at a remoter date than that which many representatives of old families are known to plume themselves on.

It is hardly possible to conceive anything of the sort so grotesque as this wood appears, with their branches just spreading themselves over the enormous blocks of granite among which they are intermingled and their upper lateral roots twisted around their bases, and in the most fantastic wreathings insinuated, whereon recess or interstices offered themselves. Among the oaks, a few shrub like trees of mountain ash and an immense quantity of the Fumaria clariculata, small climbing Funitory, rather a scarce plant, appeared to diversify the scene. There was however a sort of solemn awe, that pervaded it. Silence seemed to have taken up her abode in this sequestered wood, and to a supersticious mind some impression would have occurred approaching to dread or sacred horror.

I shall now advert to the circles of stone, which I have before noticed in my way from Tavistoke, near Randals stone, and which lie between this wood and Crockern Torr in abundance.

The appearance of these circles, formed of large stones, and at times connected in the manner of rude walls in a state of dilapidation has suggested the several ideas of their being sepulchres of Ancient Britons, inclosures for their flocks and herds, or houses for their residence. Had there been an opportunity, I would have ascertained the first supposition, by getting the area of them dug into. But as this did not fall within my power, I have nothing left me, but to join issue with those who have considered them, as remnants of houses and inclosures. I embrase both conjectures, from the circumstances of the different sizes of the circles, for though the major part were about 15 feet in diameter, there were several that were 60. These then I suppose were pens wherein the cattle, during the night, or very inclement weather, might be kept both safe and sheltered. It must, after a time, unavoidably have occurred to them, that to raise stone inclosures, contiguous to their own dwelling houses, would be the means of provding for them the best security.

Of this description I shall take it for granted were those large circles, generally, found contiguous to the smaller ones, and which upon the same grounds I shall consider as places of the herdsmens abode.

From the various descriptions which I have given in the course of this my Survey a strong idea must have been entertained, of the local character of Dartmoor. To a vastness of extent, which attaches to itself a degree of magnificence, the higher swells of the forest have also in themselves a peculiar trait of solemn and savage grandeur. There are but few picturesque scenes, and these are restricted solely to the rivers, and their foamy tumblings over inartificial masses of granite, rudely piled by the force of torrents on one another.

The scenery that presents itself to the eye of the beholder, wheresover it shall be cast, is in its composition grand and wild. Nothing has been here frittered or lain out on a trim or narrow scale.

On the Thursday morning soon after breakfast I took my departure from Prince Hall, and turning my horse eastward travelled on the road that led to Ashburton, having on my left a wide expanse of uncultivated Moor, and on my right a wall running parallel with the road. Not far from hence I came to Dunabridge pound, a large walled inclosure for the safe detention of cattle, just within whose gate was a rude kind of seat, over canopied by a single flat stone of considerable dimensions. Contiguous was a pot house, and in front of it Farmer Lemans well cultivated estate. Leman was at first a labourer on Dunabridge Estate at four pence per day. But scraping up by the severest economy a small sum he purchased an ewe, then two, in process of time a cow, all of which, by a natural increase, enlarged his stock. At length he became master of a new take, and by the loan of a small sum made a purchase of Dunabridge farm for £400, which by a perserverance in the same industry assisted by a keeness of understanding that led him to the best mode of improving a Moor Estate, he had more than quadrupled in its value at his desease.

At but a short distance from hence I skirted on the right a well cultured farm belonging to a man of the name of Norris. It is called Hucaby, and through it, diverging from the Ashburton road, is another which leads towards Holne. Here on the Dart which also runs through Hucaby crossing the Holne road at right angles was another of these ancient bridges. But this has been superceeded by a more safe and commodious one.

The new handsome bridge of two arches just below the ancient one, was erected in the year 1792 and I conceive was indebted for its existence to the influence of the Proprietor of Prince Hall, in whom originated not only this but almost every other improvement that of late has been effected on Dartmoor.

I pursued my way to Ashburton, at which place I arrived about an hour after noon. Here in my own house, now converted into one of the best and pleasantest inns in the West of England I took my dinner. The gardens, the walks, and the prospect here offer ample amusement for an hours idle lounge, from which the other in the centre of the Town is altogether debarred. Having taken my dinner about five I quitted Ashburton, proceeding homeward on the turnpike road leading through Bickington to Bovey Heathfield.

Drawn by T.M. Baynes. Engraved by A. Mc Clatchie.

NEW BRIDGE NEAR HOLNE.

ON THE DART

London, R. Jennings, & W. Chaplin, 62, Cheapside, 1830.

LYDFORD CASCADE.

Tavistock's boundaries in 1850 included quite considerable tracts of moorland and thrived as much on the proceeds of mining as on farming. Its weekly market was held each Friday and was one of the largest in the county for corn and slaughtered sheep, swine etc. and in addition there were nine cattle fairs held each year. The Duke of Bedford who owned most of Tavistock redeveloped much of the old centre of the town around 1848, and amongst the earliest buildings was the corn market in 1839, and later a Market House in which are still found butchers, greengrocers, and others selling fresh farm produce. The market has proved to be a more lasting benefit than copper and tin, and the redevelopment which also included a new Guildhall is particularly attractive. The development used Hurdwick stone, a local green coloured stone which has weathered well. Its colouring, scale and style helps to make the centre of Tavistock outstanding.

There was considerable development in the town in the early years of the Victorian period. Perhaps the most interesting was the model cottages which the Duke of Bedford built for the many workers employed in his mining ventures. A good number of the 7000 inhabitants of Tavistock were employed in the various mines opened up in the neighbourhood. Copper, tin and lead were mined from four workings, called the Devonshire Great Consols, or Wheal Maria, Bedford United, Tavy Consols and Wheal Russell. All were opened between 1845-50 and shares for the Great Consols were initially sold at £1 and by 1850 fetched £200 each. This mine employed 1100 workers and produced 1350 tons of ore each month in its hayday. By the end of the Century the mines were closed.

In 1817 trade between Tavistock and the navigable part of the Tamar had been encouraged by the completion of a canal. In its quiet fashion it was a monumental piece of engineering. At Morwellham quay the Dartington Trust have restored the various Victorian buildings and quays and run it as a museum.

The new Guildhall built by the Duke of Bedford was used for Petty Session and County Court and included within its precincts a police station and six cells. It also included a fire station, and over the nearby Abbey-Gateway were the rooms of the literary and philosophical society called the Tavistock Institution which had been established in 1828, the library of an earlier date and a museum. The literary and educational opportunities in the town were widened further in 1832 when the Mechanic's Institute was formed.

The town and its facilities had been improved greatly between 1820 and 1850, and the ancient Church of St. Eustace was thoroughly restored in 1844-5. There were four chapels belonging to the Unitarians, Independants, Wesleyans and Society of Friends in the town.

In addition new schools were built, and it was a well organised and run town under the influence of the Bedfords. It seems to have been a thriving

H. De Cort. del. 1795. G. Hollis. sc. 1817.

VIEW IN CHUDLEIGH,

DEVONSHIRE.

society, with the elderly benefiting from a variety of charitable bequests and almshouses, and the needs of most were met by a range of craftsmen and traders.

At Merrivale is a granite quarry, and the rocks and ancient circles and stone rows covering the hillside close by are probably as unchanged as the rest of the high moorland. It is interesting that the description of Cators house, which now seems to have disappeared, was not unlike the other "Dartmoor longhouses" in use on the Moor. The proprietors of Eton and some public schools would doubtless find comfort in knowing the accommodation for their pupils was equal to that of Cator's!

There is little evidence of Dunnabridge pound on the A384, although the spot is marked on the Ordnance map, and what may have been the "pot house" lies above the road, whilst Dunnabridge Farm which provides bed and breakfast is below on the valley side. This wild and rugged country is just as grand as described. Huccaby is not far distant from Dunnacombe and is probably 400 years old. It has been substantially modernised over the years but continues the farming tradition. Newbridge is a well patronised picnic site with a carpark nearby, a useful spot to start walks on the moor.

When Swete stayed at Ashburton it was a neat market town of no more than 3000 inhabitants, which increased by 800 over the next fifty years. Its growth might have been more but for the decline of the serge and blanket manufactory. This misfortune was similar to that experienced in Tavistock, although the compensating employment in mining was not so great, although in 1850 there were several tin and copper mines in the vicinity.

The A38 now bypasses the town and relieves it of considerable traffic which once passed through it from Plymouth to Exeter. There used to be fourteen inns or taverns in 1850 and it is equally well-provided today. It is an attractive town which has grown relatively little in recent times. The main road dips and curves, with attractive buildings, mostly with early Victorian fronts, interspersed with even older property, lining the pavement edge. The River Ashburn runs through it in a delightful manner adding spice and interest to the old buildings by its side. Some of the buildings have slate hanging, and one, the House of Cards in North Street, is painted to pick out the pattern of hearts, clubs, diamonds and spades in its facade. It keeps the feeling of a small market town, with small shops and unlikely nooks and crannies that embody the accidents of history and its ancient past. There are surprises like the magnificent Methodist Chapel with pediment and pillars, and for the railway enthusiasts there is a much altered Brunel station.

Drawn by T. M. Baynes. Engraved by W. Deeble.

THE MARKET PLACE, ASHBURTON.

London, Published by Robert Jennings, 62, Cheapside, Sep. 1, 1829.

LEFT: A STONE ROW, MERRIVALE

6. West Devon

by the Reverend John Swete

On the 19th September 1796, accompanied by Mrs. S. and our two youngest children in the chaise, I left Oxton on horseback, with the view of paying visits which had been long in agitation to several of our friends in the Western part of the County.

We gained the turnpike at Teignbridge which though a structure of modern date, there is some reason to think, has been erected on the fragments of arches much older, possibly Roman. Having just passed over this bridge, which about mid part is crossed by Mr. Templers canal, which though in a state of progression has yet far to advance before it can be completed. We soon after came to Newton Bushel and to Newton Abbot separated from each other by the little River Leman.

Those being left behind, we had a very pleasant country to pass through the whole way to Totnes. The mouldering towers of Berry Castle rivitted my eye during the whole of the ride that they were in view.

The dusky harbinger of night had drawn her thin veil through the air, and by the time that we reached the town of Totnes had so wrapped every thing in darkness that we were able to discern the Seven Stars only by the aid of a lamp. Under the influence of this constellation we were accommodated to our hearts content and I would never wish to be under the temporary dominions of more propitious stars.

The following morning I strolled to the Castle where there is a very picturesque assemblage of objects between the bowling green, and not far from the Quarry. The tide was flowing and had filled up a wide ditch which communicated with the River. The distant appearance of the castle groves, and the fine tower was a rich and pleasing background, whilst in the front nothing could be happier circumstanced than the old lime kiln and its rural accompaniments.

The scenery at this part of the town, when the Dart was full was of the most beautiful nature, the passing vessels and boats gave animation to the landscape on its banks, which in whatever point it was viewed was of that cast with which a Swanevelt or a Vandermeer would have been delighted.

At 11 we recommenced our journey.

Totnes, Devon

NEWTON — *From Knowle Hill.*

The Old Roman Road is now part of the A380 which passes across Haldon through the coniferous woodlands of the Forestry Commission, and shortly after through a magnificent avenue of beech that arch over the road. The nature of the road has changed and the canal Swete saw in the making was completed, flourished with the transport of granite and ball clay, and has fallen into ruin, although there are still traces to be found.

The two separated towns of Newton Abbot and Newton Bushel had coalesced by 1850 when there were 4000 living in this bustling market town.

The South Devon Railway arrived by 1846 and some very fine building had already taken place. The feeling of solid mid Victorian prosperity was consolidated by the expansion that took place after its coming with villa development around Courtenay Park, and on the hills around the town. In spite of recent crunching changes wrought by road improvements at Highweek Street and Newfoundland Way, and the building of a central multi-storey car park, it is an attractive town which in its wealth of elegant houses can rival Torquay. It has grown ten times the size it was in 1800 and now houses 20,000 people but still keeps its traditional market which has a colourful vitality. Bradley Manor is a National Trust property open to the public and Ford House to the south east of the town, an elegant Elizabethan manor, is in the hands of the District Council.

By 1850 there were all the usual facilities, a Ball Room for public meetings, a Mechanics Institution, News Room, a Savings Bank, several Provident and Friendly Societies, National and British Schools and half a dozen non conformist churches or chapels. There was of course the Gas Works constructed in 1839 and two banks, the Devon and Cornwall and Watts and Co. With twenty hotels or traverns and all the trades to be found as well as a good number of shops it was a thriving centre.

Berry Castle is one of the most beautiful ruins in Devon, whilst Totnes embodies the best of the picturesque qualities found in the small towns of the County. The buildings in High Street and Fore Street, the main narrow shopping street of the town, which slopes down to the Plains, is spanned by East Gate halfway down, and has as fine an assemblage of Elizabethan merchants' houses as can be found anywhere. It is evidently just as attractive as it was 150 years ago. The cattle market is held on the industrial estate close to the river and that established in 1848 at the top end of the town is mainly used for car parking. The medieval bridge was replaced by a new and pleasant stone bridge in 1828. Ships still bring trade to the town mainly through Reeves, a timber merchant, but some of the stone warehouses familiar to Swete now urgently need repair. The Seven Stars serves travellers with excellent food and drink, a wholesome tradition common to a number of excellent public houses in the town.

At Ivy bridge in particular, whose local charms are so dependant on the quantity of water in the river, all was foam and uproar. The torrent dashed over the huge rounded masses of granite which lay in its channel and whilst a spray arose in thick volumes, the listening ear was rent with its thundering sounds. We had but passed over the Bridge when we quitted the public road, taking one in a direct line before us. I saw not an object to attract my notice and hasten to close the detail of a most unpleasant ride, at the termination of which I found myself at the door of my friend the Reverend Duke Yonge and Cornwood vicarage.

The next morning the weather being fine, though it had continued during the whole night tempestuous, under his escort I mounted to reconnoitre the face of the country. . . . Nor was the Yealm without its attractions. Where brought up by the blocks of granite or by transverse ledges of natural rock, its face was smooth and its current was scarcely seen to glide, but when in its descending channels its waters were obstructed by the rock, or by a tree that had fallen earthward, rapid and impetuous it tumbled over every obstacle in its way, and foaming as it were with rage, rushed violently down the glen. Of this nature, correspondent in all its parts with the fine accompaniment of hills, woods, and single trees, was the scene.

We, from the summit of Stall Down, turned our eyes towards the more remote parts of the County, and in the most southern point we had a delightful catch of the environs of Plymouth, recognising with ease the beautiful hill and creasting woods of Mount Egecumbe, and the Sound, in which we could without the aid of glasses distinguish ships as they lay at anchor.

At about a mile distance on the left, surrounded by as wild a scenery as moors and rocks could compose appeared Harford Church, contiguous to it was a small hamlet and a house, called Hall, which was built by Colonel Chudleigh, father to the late famous Dutchess of Kingston, as a hunting seat.

As we rode to the verge of Henlake Down we had a commanding view of Blatchford, and Cornwood, and took in the whole of the narrow valley through which the Yealm ran, which was enriched by a profusion of woods and enlivened bright verdure.

On our return to Cornwood, we presently came to an old mansion, similar in its style to that of Wisdom. It was now in the hands of a farmer, though its slated roof, mullioned windows and pillars of entrance bespoke it to have been of greater consequence in former times; the space between this and Slade was but short.

To the beginning of the 17th century Slade continued in the name

J Farington, Esqr R.A. F. Nash sculp.

View of Berry Pomeroy Castle.

Published, May 1. 1822, by T. Cadell, Strand, London.

of Cole at which time it was sold to a Savery, in which family it was purchased by old Spurrel, who in the commencement of life was a butcher of the lowest class, but by indefatigable industry, scraping up some cash, became enabled to make contracts with Government, and for a lengthened period, accumulated vast sums of money, by supplying the Victualling Office, by the purchase of sailors tickets, and by providing an immense number of horses for the use of the Dockyard at Plymouth.

Possessed of opulence he altered not his mode of living, his table, his dress, his house, were the same, all of them mean. Exclusive of the pleasure of accumulation he knew not enjoyment and even to the last gasp, to add to his wealth, he went through drudgery and meaness, which to most other persons whose circumstances were far from affluent would have been insupportable.

On his decease the bulk of his fortune devolved to a person of the name of Pode, his great nephew, who has fixed upon Slade as his place of residence, and as the ancient mansion was in no style and inconvenient, a new one is to be erected.

Whatever pleasures there were at Ivybridge seem to have been lost in a dreary and tiresome ride. The ancient bridge on the Old Exeter Road is picturesque and the river still rushes through its attractive valley through a substantial modern town. By 1850 Ivybridge had grown into a large and respectable village with many neat houses, and three large inns able to satisfy the requirements of Plymothians wishing to spend a weekend in the country. There were also two paper mills, a corn mill, good shops, a tannery and a leather manufactory, a church and two chapels. Today most of its population depend on Plymouth for their employment.

Cornwood and the nearby hamlets of Lutton and Yondertown have grown rather more than Harford in recent years, and none of them are especially picturesque. At Cornwood there is a small but attractive square with a granite cross and one or two buildings of considerable age, probably dating from Elizabethan times. Duke Yonge remained the vicar here between 1793 and 1824 and provided a school and house for the school teacher, in 1818. This was replaced by a National School in 1859 where children are still taught. The old vicarage is on vicarage road below Wisdome and the little single span bridge, as attractive as one might imagine. Slade, Blatchford and Welcome are little changed, the latter, hard by the road to Torr and the Moor's edge. Delamore hidden in mature grounds on the edge of the village and close to the sloping cricket ground was rebuilt in 1859.

Eulogies about the countryside near Cornwood are still well deserved and to sample the pleasure of John Swete's ride over Stall Moor it is worth walking onto it from the New Wastes. From here, as one walks across the heather and ling, there is a view of Cornwood and the wood studded combes around it. Following round towards the west, above the head of the Erme, to a trig point at over 1,600 feet, one sees Plymouth Sound, with vessels at anchor behind the breakwater, Cornwall further to the west, and much of the South Hams and its coastline to the south, whilst northwood are the rolling hills towards Princetown, and to the east the downs of Brent Moor. Butterflies of all kinds, are common in summer, and ravens and buzzards not unusual where sheep, black cattle, and Dartmoor ponies wander freely. Only after reaching Penns Beacon Cairn is the scene obviously changed. The nearby china clay workings seen below on Shaugh Moor, seem in danger of gouging out half the parish and smothering the other half with high tipped white sandy waste.

The Church of St. Michaels at Cornwood is a neat little church dating from the 15th Century and earlier, and renovated substantially before 1850. There are various memorial tablets but its attraction lies with its granite pillars which appear remarkably light and crisp belying their solid qualities.

Drawn by G.B. Campion. Engraved by Henry Wallis.

IVY BRIDGE, DEVON

London. Published by R. Jennings & W. Chaplin 62, Cheapside.

OLD IVY BRIDGE

The church of Cornwood, a low building and surrounded by a few mean houses, was at our left as we passed on towards the vicarage, where after a most amusing ride we dismouted somewhat before dinner.

To the old house, my friend had erected in front, a new one on a similar construction with that which he had before built at Otterton. From two excellent rooms he had command of an exceedingly rural and pleasing landscape. We left Cornwood that we might proceed further towards the west and pay out next visit to our friends at Swilly. Having expressed a wish to explore some of the beauties of the River Plym, my kind host offered to be my escort.

Having passed by the Church which lay 3 parts of a mile from the vicarage, turning round it westward we had a view of the front of a new house, lately erected by Mr. Hayes. The place is called Dallymore, and on this site was an ancient building which Risdon calls "the curious contrived house of De la more – built by Cole". The situation was high and the prospect extended chiefly over downs, was wild and bleak. Over these downs our road led us, whose pasture and locality seemed to call loudly for cultivation.

The notion I had conceived of the probable improvement that might be made on these lands, was neither vague, nor speculative, for we soon after came in the vicinity of an hamlet called Cholwich Town, and I was soon informed that the farmer who rented it had lately inclosed a portion or two, which after burn beating, had produced him two good crops of turnip and wheat, which had amply repaid his toil and his expense.

By a gate we were let from these commons into Toort or Torch Moor where in are a number of circles, and stones erect. Quitting these rude monuments of Ancient Superstition, we travelled for some time over wild moors, now and then upon patches of the finest possible roads which had been formed of decomposed granite and having northwards a view of several of the Alpine tors of Dartmoor. On the slope of the hill I perceived a group of stones which at a distance had much the appearance of a cromlech [*This was Hawks Tor on Shaugh Moor*].

The view from the karn was extensive and highly diversified. Towards the north, the eye passing over a vast expanse of down found a magnificent boudery in Dartmoor, rising high and wild with its craggy piles amongst which Hessary Tor, on its Western extremity was most conspicuous, and detached from the moor by a few miles, Brent Tor rising as a Mountain came in the midst of a plain whose apex was formed by a church and its tower.

Ranging in a circuit southward the chief object of attraction, was the church of Shaugh, which was well discriminated, as being seated near the foot of the Down on which we were, but the most beautiful part of the prospect was that which was comprised by the Sound of Plymouth which appeared as a vast brilliant sea in the dark mass of Mount Edgecumbe and the other surrounding hills. We could directly perceive the ships riding at anchor; but this part of the scenery brought with it no inconsiderable alloy – for it was impossible not to recollect, and recollecting, not to lament that the Amphion, of whose fatal loss we had received last evening the report.

We began our descent from Hawks Tor, for so the pile of rocks is called over the remaining part of the Moor, which was thick studded with blocks of granite, towards the hamlet and church of Shaugh. Amongst a few scattered houses of a mean cast I was surprised to find a tower of the most elegant workmanship which was decorated with fretted pinacles similar to the tower of Plympton Mary.

We reached the Bridge, and from its height had the power of looking over the tops of a fine woodland expanse, and of beholding the church of Bickleigh, which was a considerable enrichment to the landscape.

The River rushed rapidly down its descending channel, and its dashing sound reverberated from the woods and rocky hills. A farm house also, whose foundations were of the living rock, rose high at the western end, and being covered with a like profusion of pendulous ivy contributed its part to complete the wild beauty of the picture. The River which had thus broken upon us at once with its artless charms was the Plym which here joins with the Mew.

Reluncantly quitting the scene of enchantment, having crossed the bridge, instead of ascending the hilly road before us, which would have conducted us to the village and church of Bickleigh, we took one, which by a quick flexure to the left, led us through the lower grounds, passing through water lanes and by a farm house and through, after two mile brought us to Bickleigh Bridge.

The scenery had now assumed around the River a milder cast, the water flowed gently through a single arch. The ledges of rock which formed the banks were no longer rounded and detached blocks of granite, but a fixed and continuous stratum of schist.

Passing on by the riverside nothing could be more delightful than the scenery. At every step some diversification of woodland beauties, occurred, and at one spot in particular where Cann Quarry became a conspicuous object the features of the landscape rose above all power of description.

Drawn by W. Westall A.R.A. Engraved by Edw.d Finden.

SHAUGH BRIDGE.

RIVER PLYM, DEVONSHIRE.

Published by Charles Tilt, 86 Fleet Street, London, 1829.

The ride was most charmingly diversified, by alternate rising and falling. At one time the beaten road ran smoothly, through one of those beautiful little straights of sod, the river roaring on the left and the woods hanging high on the right, presenting a most pleasing style of forest scenery.

We now joined the public road which conducted us through a depth of wood to Plym Bridge. Everything was picturesque. Woods rose high above, spreading themselves richly over the hills, whilst around the bridge itself there are goups and groves of oak and elms, which by their bulk demonstrated that they were "sons of other times".

With the low grounds I left these beauties of the close woodland landscape, for on ascending a hill and coming within sight of Leigham, an estate lately purchased of Admiral MacBride by Addis Archer, the view opened by a considerable extent, not without taking in many of the peculiar charms of the neighbourhood.

The traveller is not only gratified with the view of a number of gentlemen's seats, happily placed on both sides, but has for a considerable way an open prospect of Plymouth and Dock, of Mount Edgcumbe and the Sound.

At a turnpike gate turning to the right into the road leading to Saltash about four I reached my friend Furneaux's house at Swilly where I found Mrs. S. and the children, who had gained their journeys end two hours before me.

Within a few fields of Swilly, lying westward of it in a narrow valley at the head of a creak communicating with the estuary of the Tamar, some little way higher up than the dockyard, is Ford. The house is of an old cast and embosomed in groves of Elms, and belongs to Mrs. Crode a relative of Mr. Furneaux. We passed down the side of the Creek till we came to the grounds of Mrs. Crode. The chief use to which Mrs. Crode applies her ground is that of finding sustenance for about four score horses, with which by contract she supplies the Dockyard. A very lucrative employment it seems, by which this old lady, treading in the steps of her great predecessor Spurle is amassing for her heirs, future squires and sherriffs, immense wealth.

The want of confidence as to personal security must greatly detract from the beauty of the finest spot that Ford enjoys in such a neighbourhood. Nothing but habit I should think, could render anyone so heedless of his safety as to be upon the road of the environs of Plymouth and the Dockyard at night. To warrant such apprehensions, nothing more will be needed than an inspection of the list of prisoners annually tried at the assizes in Exeter, and we shall find that there are a greater number of persons committed to gaol, and that for crimes of deepest die, for murder, burglery, highway robberies etc, from Plymouth and its vicinity, than from all the other parts of the County of Devon put together.

I came at length to the environs of Stonehouse where every object, animate and inanimate was dressed "en militaire". I sat myself down on a projecting crag with an intent more minutely to contemplate the varied charms of the scenery which I had before me, but a bustle occasioned by a group of men at some little distance eagerly endeavouring to drag somewhat from the surge destroyed in an instant all my proposed enjoyment for I conceived that their efforts were used to drag from the waves the mangled corpse of someone who had suffered death by the explosion of the Amphion. The Amphion was a Frigate of 32 guns, commanded by Captain Israel Pellew, brother of the gallant Sir Edward, and was just returned from a cruise to refit.

About 4 oclock in the afternoon the fore magazine took fire and blew up with a most dreadful explosion. In consequence this part of the ship was shivered to atoms and what was left sank almost instantly in 12 fathoms of water.

The ships company and the visitors on board at the time, women chiefly, are from the best accounts stated at near 250, out of which number, according to the most accurate returns that have been made, only 37 men and two women have been saved, and some of these severely injured.

A party of shipwrights and other belonging to the Yard in the act of cutting away such of the Amphion upper works and stores, as the reflux of the tide would enable them to get at, discovered the body of a woman jammed under the half deck, which they ineffectually endeavoured to get out, presently after, a biscuit bag, apparently full, was observed, which on inspection was found to contain a considerable quantity of bread, and about 30 lbs of gunpowder. Hence it may be inferred that an illicit traffic of the ammunication of the ship had been on foot at the time of the disaster, and that to it, and it alone, is to be attributed the dreadful catastrophe.

From Swilly on Tuesday morning to Tamerton Foliot, a sequestered village situated on the slope of a hill, declining towards a creek, formed by the Tamar near its junction with the Tavy. Mr. Richards was the curate of the Parish and receiving us in a neat cottage contiguous to the Church, exercised towards us the most hospitable attentions.

On the following morning we rode to Warley, the seat of Radcliffe Esq., through the aged groves of oak and ash, which had been planted to protect the Mansion from the West and northern blasts, we

J.H. Williams, Plymouth

Tamerton Foliot.

passed to a projecting point into the Tavy, where was a boat and a prospect room. The beauty of this spot, comprised in its own embosoming woods, which were washed by the river ride, of attraction with the embellishment of the lawns and groves of Marystow.

In the hands of a man of taste Warley might become one of the first spots in the County, half encircled by the waters of the Tamar and Tavy, commanding the picturesque grounds of Marystow, the towns of Saltash and Beer Ferris it is not possible to ascertain to what an high degree of eminance it may be brought.

Hawks Tor on Shaugh Moor has escaped the vast mounds of white sand that now rise close by, although Cholwich Town, an outstanding Elizabethan farmhouse, stands under its shadow. It is in an area where ancient stones are thickly scattered and these obviously delighted the diarist speculating upon their heathen significance. Consideration by modern archaeologists have still left them puzzles of antiquity suitable for harmless speculations.

Hessary Tor is easily recognised by the tall wireless mast that sits on its sumit, whilst St Michael Church on Brentor is just as prominent, and was fully restored in 1889-1890.

By contrast to the exposed walking on the Moor, Bickleigh Vale is a delightfully sheltered and cosy valley. At its head and a little to the east of the village of Shaugh Prior is the craggy mass of the Dewerstone Rock . By 1850 there were about 700 living in the Parish, and the little huddle of houses around the Church with its distinctive tower was probably little altered. There are rather more houses today, a petrol filling station and a pub.

Above Shaugh Bridge where the Plym and Meavy meet is an ancient plantation of Oak which over the years have become festooned with lichen, a sure sign of clear air! This is National Trust land, and there are similar attractive hard wood acres around the fourteenth-century Plym bridge. Swete travelled down the western side of the valley which remains an especially attractive woodland walk. From Shaugh Bridge it descends southwards to Bickleigh bridge through meadow lands with gently rising valley sides, steeper on the east bank. After Bickleigh Bridge the well wooded valley becomes narrower with steeper sides until it broadens out again below Plym Bridge. There is still much hard wood within the valley, oak, ash and alder as well as areas of scrub, especially along the west bank. There has however been quite extensive coniferous planting at Cann Wood and Great Shaugh on the eastern bank, Trill wood in the south and in the north Squares Wood.

T. Allom   Wm Le Petit

MARISTOW, DEVONSHIRE.

THE SEAT OF SIR RALPH LOPEZ, BART

FISHER, SON & Co LONDON, 1832.

T. Allom. W. Le Petit.

CARN QUARRY, BICKLEIGH VALE, DEVONSHIRE.

FISHER, SON, & C° LONDON, 1831.

It would be easy to imagine the valley as a quiet place unhurried and untouched for the past 150 years but between 1800 and 1855 Cann Quarry below Cann Weir Viaduct was in full production of slate. A canal was built to carry the slate to Marsh Mills and did so until 1835 when it was replaced by a tramway built along the tow path. After this the canal was used only as a mill leat.

How busy it was can be judged by the remains of railways and tramways which in addition to that from Cann Quarry passed through this striking landscape of woodlands and swift flowing water. The Great Western Railway completed a branch line with spectacular viaducts, through it in 1859. The Plymouth and Dartmoor Railway tramway came earlier in 1827 and was twenty five miles long carrying granite from the Moor. Its route can be followed along the western side of the Vale, skirting the valley of Glen Holt.

The Lee Moor Tramway which was a branch line to the South Devon and Tavistock Railway, opened in 1854 to carry china clay from Lee Moor to Cattewater Quay in Plymouth. The whole tramway above Marsh Mills stopped working in 1947. In 1961 a pipeline carrying china clay suspended in water was laid along its path.

The Lee Moor Tramway, the Great Western Railway, the Cann Quarry Canal and Tramway all meet south of Plym Bridge. None are now used, but all can be traced through Bickleigh Vale.

In the expansion of Plymouth, the estates of Ford and Swilly have been engulfed by relatively modern development, and the picturesque beauty of their grounds have been lost beneath concrete and tarmac.

Mount Edgecumbe is owned by the Plymouth City Council and its garden presents a mature and attractive face to the City and is used as a country park. Warleigh house is set amongst mature grounds planted shortly after Swete saw it, and mature woodland at Warleigh point is run by the Devon Trust for Nature Conservation as a nature reserve.

Maristow was built in 1740 for the Heywoods who remained, until it was sold by heiresses in 1798 to the Lopes family (Lord Roborough), who have owned it ever since. It has recently been gutted by fire and its future has been in some doubt, whilst in the same way Budshead Barn was destroyed by fire and not rebuilt.

The next morning we quitted Swilly with the intention of passing a day with Reverend James Yonge at his seat of Puslinch.

By way of diversifying my ride I made a circuit through the town of Plymouth, crossing again on my approach to it, the leat, or artificial brook, which taken from the River Mew, near its source in one of the wild vallies of Dartmoor, not only affords a most abundant supply of water to Plymouth, but passing in its course from mountains over a track of high ground, to an extent of near twenty miles, contributes much to their value, in that it slakes the thirst of cattle kept on them. For its use, in watering lands, there is an absolute prohibition. The advantages of this leat have been so great, that the Government have been instigated to procure similar ones for the town of Dock and the shipping there, this has been begone several years and is nearly completed.

WARLEIGH HOUSE

T. Allom. Wm Le Petit.

WARLEGH HOUSE, DEVONSHIRE.

THE SEAT OF WALTER RADCLIFFE, ESQ.

7. Plymouth

by Miss Mary Cornish

Swete's visit to Plymouth in 1795 as part of his Western tour provides little detail of the three towns of Plymouth, Stonehouse and Dock, although the environs were apparently very attractive.

A later account during 1824 by Mary Cornish who lived in Sidmouth and travelled about the County visiting friends and relatives, records a trip to Plymouth in more peaceful times a decade after the war with France was over.

1824
October

11th
Left Blackhall early this morning for Plymouth, stopped at Ivybridge and leaving the carriage and horses there went on to Cornwood to see the Oxnams who are lately settled there. Found them all at home and met with a kind reception. The situation of Cornwood is beautiful and the garden belonging to the parsonage the prettiest thing I ever saw – but my head was in sad confusion and I could hardly enjoy anything. Returned to Ivybridge and then went on to Plymouth. When we arrived (at Mrs. Rayners) about 8 o clock.
12th
Went in Mr. Arthurs yacht to see the Breakwater. Wonderful effort of art to oppose Nature, which few minds could have conceived. I never enjoyed anything more than the sail – its been quite a gale of wind and the sea was so rough that the boat went over the waves like lightning and I could compare it to nothing but to riding at full gallop on the back of a very high horse. The one difference was that one was an active, the other a passive pleasure. My mind has more equal to the enjoyment of the waters today, though the other is I think superior. We went upon the breakwater and walked the whole length of it.
13th
Went again on the water and went on board the Britannia, the flag ship, which is now stationed here, of 120 guns. I had never been aboard any ship before except the Asia East Indiaman in which Frederick Shore went to India, and that could give little or no idea of the ship here. It was all new to me, and I never was more delighted or surprised by anything I ever saw before. The appearance of the ship as we approached her in the little boat was almost overwhelming. She seemed like a great mountain ready to crush us. – When we came on board all the men were at duties, and the noise and bustle was very great. I seemed to be in a little world where all was novelty and unlike anything I had ever seen before. I went all over the ship, and Captain Arthur who accompanied us explained everything to me, and answered all my various questions with great patience and kindness. It would take some time indeed really to comprehend all the different parts of their great machine, and yet there is a great simplicity about it too in appearance. What struck me very much was that there was not a single object present to our view that did not convey some idea either of utility, action, or manly and vigorous exertion. There was sense in everything. The Admirals and Captains apartments discovered some little attempts at luxury and superfluity, but the greater part of the ship even of their furniture had been made on board the ship. I went into every part of the ship even into the magazine. The carpenters and gunners room were extremely well arranged. The most perfect order and neatness pervaded every part. I had no idea so small a space could have enclosed such variety of new ideas as I gained by this sight. I have never been more gratified than I can describe and think it will be very long before I shall see anything which as a sight can be compared with a ship. We dined at Mr. Arthurs at Norley House and in the evening I went to a Ball with Papa and John Mayon that I might have an opportunity of seeing the Ballroom to the best advantage. I never saw such a brilliant Ball before. The number of Military and Naval officers in full uniform made it look very splendid and I here saw a great many persons of high rank in the room. I danced the whole evening as we came home a little after twelve. Was less fatigued than I expected after all the events of the day and was very much amused – we also saw the Athenaeum this morning which must be a very useful institution.
14th
Left Plymouth about two oclock, highly gratified with all we saw and the very kind and friendly attention of Mrs. Rayner and her sisters. John is I think much relieved we had a fine day. The scenery from Plymouth to Plympton is beautiful and again from there to Ivybridge. Arrived at Blackhall about 3 and then took a walk with Esther along the boarders of the river which flows through the grounds.

T. Allom. J. Thomas.

ROYAL THEATRE, AND ATHENÆUM.

FISHER, SON, & Co. LONDON. 1832.

Mary Cornish could well have taken with her on her visit to Plymouth a suitable guide of 1823 like The Tourist's Companion: being a Guide to the Towns of Plymouth, Plymouth Dock, Stonehouse, Morice Town, Stoke and their Vicinities. *Like many guides of this period it produced a full account of the virtues and facilities but did not shirk outright criticism of some of the conditions to be found, which since guides generally dwelt more on the favourable aspects than the blemishes, suggests that substantial areas of Plymouth were insanitary slums.*

PLYMOUTH
from *The Tourist's Companion*

Sometimes called Sutton, alias South Town, (whence probably the name of Sutton Pool), and seems to have consisted heretofore of two parts, there being mention made of Sutton Vautort and Sutton Prior. The laylord thereof left his name to the one; and Plymton Prior, to whom a good part of it appertained, left his an adjunct to the other. At present it is generally understood by all who have not obtained an acquaintance with it by personal observation, to consist of one town; and as many inconveniences result from this misapprehension, it becomes necessary to explain that, though it is in a political point of view, as a naval arsenal, but one place; yet that in fact, it consists of the towns enumerated in the title-page, namely – Plymouth, Dock, Stonehouse, Morice-town, and Stoke.

Plymouth, being a corporate town, is governed by its own magistrates, namely – a mayor, the mayor of the preceeding year, who is denominated the justice, a recorder, and the two senior members of the bench of aldermen.

The corporation is known by the legal style of "The mayor and commonalty of the borough of Plymouth," but by the grant of several characters from different kings and queens of this realm, there are the following officers in the body, viz. twelve aldermen, twenty-four common council men, a town clerk, and coroner.

The following subordinate officers are appointed by the mayor to execute his commands, and wait in attendance on him, viz. a chamberlain, two serjeants at mace, and three town corporals.

The magistrates are empowered by charter to hold a general sessions of the peace, after the four feasts of Lady-day, Midsummer, Michaelmas, and Christmas, where offences, not amounting to capital punishments, are capable of being tried. The streets of the town are in general ill constructed, narrow, if irregular, and some of them steep; many of the by-streets are particularly filthy, especially those through which the water of the town is permitted to flow, from a mistaken notion of its contributing to the cleanliness of them; but the effects produced by it are diametrically opposite, for the lower order of inhabitants, trusting to this stream of water removing all annoyances, are in the habit of throwing into the street every description of offensive matter. Most of the streets are paved; some of them, however, in the skirts of the town, still remain unpaved, which renders them vastly inconvenient. The streets are lighted from Michaelmas to lady-day, and the town has of late years had a more perfect night watch established than formerly; the watchmen are now stationed in boxes in different parts of the town. The constables who visit the different posts during the night, are at other times stationed at the watchhouse in the Guildhall, where persons wishing to give any public alarm from the occurrence of fire, robbery, or housebreaking, should instantly resort; and with respect to the latter cases, instant information should be given to the magistrates, who will direct immediate enquiry to be made by

DEVONPORT AND DOCK YARD
by J. M. W. Turner, R.A.

LEFT: THE BARBICAN

the town serjeants, and other police officers; for the means of detection are often lost by the least delay.

The watch and officers of police, after ten o'clock, are, however, vigilant; and the streets are as quiet as in any country town.

The inhabitants of the town are well supplied with fresh water, and are indebted for it to the famous Sir Francis Drake, by whose skill and exertion it was brought in a channel from the river Mew, on the borders of Dartmoor, by a devious course of nearly twenty-four miles. Prior to this period they had to rely wholly on the springs of the town, which afforded an inadequate supply when the town increased in size and population. This water has ever been vested in the mayor and commonalty, who grant leases of it to the proprietors of houses for twenty-one years upon paying a fine of three pounds thirteen shillings and sixpence, and an annual rent of twelve shillings per annum. Persons who use more water than private families, pay one pound four shillings per annum. There are several public conduits in the town, where the poor are accommodated with the water gratuitously. Another advantage attending the bringing of this water to the town, was its enabling the corporation to erect corn-mills, at which part of the flour used in the town is ground; and there are several manufactories worked by this stream.

The author admits that there were surprisingly few local seafaring men of distinction, and also suggests that there are relatively few artists of distinction as well, whilst the shops of sculptors in the town were only worthy of visiting to see the various sorts of marble available locally.

The fine arts are likely, however, to meet support, by the establishment of an athenaeum; in which an annual exhibition of paintings takes place; and a prominent feature of the society, by whom it is undertaken, is to stimulate circulation, by giving preference to the productions of native artists. In conjunction with the Public Library and this Institution, both of which aim at the elevation of Plymouth, and have concentrated together into a focus for the general ability of the place, for the beneficial purpose of diffusing information more widely, this endeavour to foster indigenous talent, and give it an opportunity of expanding, cannot fail, if properly appreciated, to impart to Plymouth a superior degree of moral attainment.

Music is said to be much in vogue here: there are concerts and balls in the winter, but no permanent musical establishments. During some winters there are public concerts; at others there are private associations; at both of which the instrumental and vocal music of a description little above mediocrity.

With respect to literature, in general it is not to be expected to prevail much in a sea-port, amidst the enterprise of commercial speculations; and though Liverpool has had a Currie, and a Roscoe, these are hitherto unusual combinations. We are happy, however, to be able to notice some recent instances, which shew that a taste for it is not wanting, and efforts to shew itself have been manifested in the erection of a public library in Cornwall-street. This institution owes its foundation to George Eastlake, Esq. who has been indefatigable in his exertions to promote it. Several societies of gentlemen, in which new and periodical publications are circulated, have long existed here; and the medical gentlemen have a club, where books connected with the science of medicine only, are introduced. A Peace Society is established, of which W. Prideaux, Esq. is treasurer; and during the last year, a society called the Plymouth Religious Tract Society, was also established, for the purpose of distributing religious tracts to the poor, of which R. Derry, Esq. is treasurer. There are likewise several circulating libraries. The number of booksellers is considerable. There are several printing presses in the town, but they are usually employed in printing advertisements and mercantile papers. A newspaper has been established here, which is published every Thursday morning, named "The Plymouth and Plymouth Dock Journal". Another paper, entitled "The Devonshire Freeholder," is published and has also an establishment formed at Exeter, in order to promote a more general circulation in the north and eastern parts of Devonshire, and for the attainment of local information of the county, which it usually embraces.

A stranger is much more struck in going through the town, with the apparent want of dwelling-houses for the more opulent inhabitants; for, excepting about the part of the town called Frankfort-place, Brunswick-terrace, George-street, and a few others, but they are so concealed in bye-streets and lanes, or situated in the gardens of the proprietors, as not to be easily discovered, and are likewise scattered about in different parts of the town. There is no uniformity preserved in the buildings in any of the streets, except a few houses in Frankfort-place, Frankfort-row, George-street, and those above-mentioned; in other parts, you may be assured, that no two houses will resemble each other; indeed in this respect the inhabitants are like those in other places, for no regard is paid, when a house is to be rebuilt, to the houses adjoining, unless it be to observe cautiously, that it shall in no instance bear any affinity to its neighbour: if a house is built of brick, the adjoining one will of course be built of stone; if the one has a parapet wall, the other will have none; if the door is in the middle of one house, it must be in the side of the other; the windows must be of

T. Allom. W. Le Petit.

THE NEW VICTUALLING OFFICE, DEVIL'S POINT, PLYMOUTH.

different patterns, the stories of different heights, and the roofs by no means parallel; and finally, the wood work, if painted white in the one, is sure to be of a different colour in the next: these observations, though applicable to other towns, are most strictly just with respect to Plymouth.

Little business is in progress, no employment presents itself to the poor, who are thus without the means of subsistence for themselves and families; the workhouse overflows with tenants, and the number of distressed objects applying for relief is incredible. Some humane and charitable individuals, in order to alleviate these distresses, have at various times since the peace promoted subscriptions for the purpose of supplying food and labour for the industrious, by their relief thus aforded, Plymouth has at this time to boast of the beautiful and extensive new walk and carriage road under the Hoe, so much admired by strangers.

Within the last ten years, it may be said to have been in a progressive state of improvement, as to buildings; a new street, from Nut-street, to the West end of George-street, is nearly completed. It is also in contemplation, to erect a handsome square, to be named Cobourg-square, in memory of our much lamented Princess Charlotte, the centre of which will be adorned with a full length statue of her royal highness, from an elegant design. The new street is to pass through it, and the houses are intended to be of that respectable class, as to size and accommodation which is so much wanted in the town. The spot is most judiciously chosen, in the vicinity of the Hoe; which, for salubrity of air, and beauty of prospect cannot be excelled.

The vast population of this neighbourhood during the war, besides the military and navy, and supplies drawn from hence for distant fleets, together with its peculiar situation, being on one side bounded by the sea, and on the other by large tracts of uncultivated country, have contributed to raise the rent of pasture land to a height unparalleled in any other part of the kingdom that we have heard of. Instances occur of ground being let for seventeen pounds an acre, clear of all rates and taxes; many instances for fifteen pounds and fourteen pounds. These exorbitant rents can no longer be obtained; the dismissal of his majesty's seamen, the disbanding of the militias with which these towns were principally garrisoned, and the consequent decrease of the population, as connected with them, having rendered the great demand for agricultural produce no longer necessary.

With respect to the public amusements in this town, the theatre is opened during a few of the summer and winter months; at the latter season, there is an assembly for dancing, held every alternate Wednesday, at the Royal Hotel. A great deal of private visiting prevails in various circles; some partaking of the fashionable dinner, at five or six o'clock, whilst others are content to meet early in the evenig, take their tea, play at cards, and retire at an early hour. There is not much dissipation among the higher classes, though private dances and concerts occasionally break in on the hours of the night. In their intercourse with each other, those who have not carriages of their own, and who refuse to use the public ones, are accommodated with sedan chairs, of which there are about six in the town.

STONEHOUSE

East Stonehouse is situated about one mile west of Plymouth, and nearly midway between that town and Dock, although the buildings in Union street almost approach those at the extremity of Plymouth. The great turnpike to the ferry at Newpassage, which is continued from Torpoint through Cornwall, passes through Stonehouse; from which circumstance, and the erection of the hospitals and barracks, it has risen, within a few years, from a small village to a handsome town. The present number of inhabitants is computed at seven thousand.

The police of Stonehouse is under the direction of Thomas Clinton Shiells, Esq., a county magistrate, resident in the town; but all complaints and other business are brought before the bench of magistrates, at their weekly sittings at the town-hall in Dock. The usual number of constables are appointed, but there are no watchmen, nor are the streets lighted at any period of the year. With the exception of the older parts of the town, the buildings are neat and handsome, and the streets straight and commodious, particularly those of Durnford-street, Emma-place, Edgcumbe-street, and Union-street. These are almost entirely occupied by genteel families, chiefly those of naval and military officers, and other persons holding situations under government. The addition of Union-street, which has taken place within the last seven years, is an improvement of the greatest importance, as the road through Fore-street is narrow and inconvenient, and the houses for the most part irregularly built; while the new road affords a spacious thoroughfare, and presents to strangers, on their entrance, a succession of neat and uniform buildings.

Drawn by H. Worsley. Engraved by T. Higham.

SUTTON POOL & CUSTOM HOUSE, PLYMOUTH.

London Published by Robert Jennings 62 Cheapside March 1 1830.

The inhabitants are supplied with water by the Dock water works, from whence it is brought by means of pipes carried across the creek; the rent of which is the same as at Dock. The only kind of commerce carried on here, are the coal and timber trades. The vessels thus employed discharge their cargoes at the quays in Stonehouse Pool. The principal quay is spacious and convenient, and the dues for landing goods, are collected by a renter. The watermen who ply for hire, resort to this quay, and like those at Plymouth, are under no regulation as to their fares. Near this is a shipwright's yard, where vessels can be drawn up and repaired.

T. Allom. H. Wal

THE BARBICAN, POOL, &c. PLYMOUTH.

FISHER, SON, & Co LONDON, 1832.

J. M. W. TURNER, R.A. DEL.T W. B. COOKE, SCULP.T

DEVONPORT.

PLYMOUTH-DOCK

Is a town of modern date, and has no pretensions to antiquity. It derives its first name from the old town of Plymouth, and the latter from the establishment of his majesty's dock-yard here, which took place towards the latter end of the reign of King William III. It is situated farther to the westward than Stonehouse, being less than a mile distant from it, and stands on a pleasant eminence, between Stonehouse creek and the harbour of Hamoaze, which is that part of the Tamar that forms the harbour here. The town has been erected on an extensive plain, in a very desirable situation, both as respects a free circulation of air, and the delightful prospects that may be seen from it in every direction.

It is perhaps, more than probable, that within the last ninety-eight years, the inhabitants have increased to ten times their number, by the accession of persons of different descriptions, who have accumulated here during the late and former wars on account of the dock-yard and shipping, and for the purpose of trade.

But a small part of St. Aubyn-street was built till toward the year 1770. The like may be observed of Chapel-street, and the other streets in that quarter, down to he present market. The date on the chapel and on Nelson's buildings at the south end are proofs of its modern foundation. The part called Pembroke-street, with the other streets in that part, are of still later origine; for about the year 1775, Liberty Field (as that part was then called) was used as a rope-walk.

Not long after, George-street was begun to be built, and the rage for extending the buildings, or the speculations of mechanics, being at that time very prevalent, Pembroke-street and Clowance-street on that side, with Mount-street and the cross streets which connect them, and Windmill-street trod so fast upon the heels of each other, that they quickly occupied the full limits of the town. The field of Windmill-hill having fallen into the hands of the lord of the manor, a considerable part of it has been removed, Duke-street and Mount-street completed, and a new avenue, (called Ker-street) with connecting lanes. Thus no ground remains to be built upon except the mill field, which we understand may probably continue many years in its present condition.

Where the market at present stands, was formerly a pond, which was filled up more than fifty years since for that purpose. The town was naturally deficient in that necessary article of life, water, and for some time the inhabitants suffered much inconvenience from an inadequate supply, being obliged to purchase it off persons who carried it about in barrels; but in the year 1792, an application was made to parliament to

Davenport.

THE STATUE OF QUEEN VICTORIA THAT BEFORE THE WAR WAS SITED ON TOP OF THE TOWN HALL (SEE OPPOSITE)

THE TOWN-HALL, COLUMN, & LIBRARY, DEVONPORT.

establish a company, called the "Plymouth-Dock Water Company," with power to bring a stream from the borders of Dartmoor to the town, a distance from the circuitous course of nearly thirty miles. This water was at first conveyed through elm pipes, but of late years cast-iron pipes have been laid down, and the dock-yard, gun-wharf, barracks, and every part of the town are constantly supplied from the reservoir near the lines on the north side of the town.

The batteries of Eastern Western King, on the peninsula from Stonehouse (after passing the garrison of Plymouth, and the guns of St. Nicholas's Island) are well situated to annoy any enemy before they can reach the strait into Barn-pool, when those on Mount Wise would be ready to give them a warm reception. Immense military works of stone are now partly erected around the town: they were, however, suspended in the year 1816, and the workmen, amounting to many hundreds discharged. It was intended to have extended the new lines the whole circuit of the old works, which, by an addition of ground, would have rendered the grand parade one of the finest in Europe, and added considerably to the effect of the military spectacles which so often occur in this town, and therefore does not admit of any increase of buildings within its lines. The superabundance of its population has rendered it necessary to have recourse to the erection of a new town without the lines, named Morice-town, from the circumstance of the whole parish wherein it is situated having been formerly the sole property of the family of Sir William Morice, Bart. as it is now of Sir John St. Aubyn, Bart. who inherits it from the Morice family, with the exception of two estates, called Ford and Swilly, the glebe, and ground purchased by government. The ancient village of Stoke has likewise of late years so much increased in size, as to warrant it being called another town.

The streets of Stoke Damerel are regular, well built, and some excellent houses with handsome fronts, have been of late years added; they neatly intersect each other at right angles; their general width is from thirty to fifty feet, and they are well paved with marble, from quarries in the neighbourhood, and they receive such a polish from the friction occasioned by the feet of passengers and the action of water, as to give them a very beautiful appearance when washed by a shower. The streets are kept much cleaner, are in general more level, as well as wider, more convenient and pleasant, than those of Plymouth.

Since 1914 Plymouth, Devonport and Stonehouse have been incorporated into the one city of Plymouth, although the local allegiances still quiver beneath the surface of what most casual observers see as a grey spread of undivided development which is the home of over 240 thousand Plymothians. Like many cities it needs the sun to bring out its more attractive assets. When the sun is shining and the sea is blue and sparkling, and the hills of Dartmoor to the north are clearly seen, it's possible to thoroughly enjoy the bustle of the fishing port, the naval craft leaving harbour and some of the nooks and crannies left from earlier times, and regret the losses of the war and the redevelopment of many of the old suburbs that followed it.

Sir Patrick Abecrombie's plan for the redevelopment of the City has resulted in a new shopping centre which is quite adequate, and uses Portland Stone and brick in a neat unspectacular fashion. It is a commendable effort to recreate much of the dignity and interest that was lost. The previous great rebuilding was between 1800 and 1850, and the most famous of those responsible was John Foulstone who set up his architectural practice in Plymouth when he was forty years old, and who worked for the next twenty years here to help make the three towns as elegant as almost anywhere in the South West. His influence started when he won a competition for building the Theatre Royal and the Royal Hotel, which were completed in the classical style in 1813. Almost all of his work has gone except the Devonport town hall, designed in 1821/2, after the style of the Parthenon at Athens. The Egyptian house standing next to it and desperately in need of repair is another of his works. Foulstone's partner George Wightwick continued the practice until 1850 and their influence over other designers and builders must have been considerable.

It is the sea that is the common bond that joins the past and present Plymouth. Whilst the bricks and mortar used to house the 90,000 living in the three towns in 1850 have largely been demolished or crumbled to decay, the wharves and quays being improved at that time have largely survived. Overseeing them is the Hoe with the Citadel to the east. The open space of the Hoe was styled "the lungs of Plymouth" in 1850 and was where everyone took their air and exercise. Carriage drives, public walks and seats were provided and the splendid sights of the Sound, Drakes Island, the Breakwater and the Mew Stone were as pleasurable then as now. The sea and estuary were common to each of the towns and these common bonds are worthy of consideration before separately cataloguing the improvements that took place in them.

The Citadel is a large fortification on the headland to the west of Sutton Pool, built of limestone and granite. It still consists of three regular and two irregular bastions. Cannon were mounted on the fort, and there were embrasures for 120 pieces on the upper parapets. The gateway with a sculpture of the royal arms and other ornamentations, like the rest of the fortifications is still there although the ditch that surrounded it, crossed by a drawbridge, has gone.

The Barbican area to the west of the Hoe with its ancient stone warehouses, shops and Tudor merchants' houses attractively edges Sutton Pool, still used by the fishing fleet but now crowded with private boats. In 1845 it was deepened and cleansed and sea walls and quays were built there. These improvements together with others were intended to provide one of the finest tidal harbours in the Kingdom. Granite and limestone with grey slate roofs offer a quaint as well as attractive view of early Victorian Plymouth. The Customs House and the square in front paved neatly with granite setts is most attractive, and enlivened by a huge colourful end of building mural, which oddly goes rather well in the area.

Mill Bay further west still is larger than Sutton Pool, and in 1850, with a pier extending from the limestone and marble quarries across the eastern side it could take vessel of 3000 tons burthen at low water. The pier was built in 1840 at a cost of over £27,000 and was bought by the Great Western Dock Co after its completion with the intention of enticing the P and O steam packets away from Southampton. Today it is used as the Cross Channel ferry terminus although passengers once embarked on ships bound for India or America and Canada here – 8,500 of them in 1850 were emigrants, all hoping for a better life.

The Hamoaze is the estuary of the River Tamar where it meets the Sound below Devonport, and it was here that many of the Royal Naval establishments were located. Rennie's Royal Victualling Yard has a striking gateway which is probably little changed since it was built. The grey stone buildings of the Royal Marine Barracks in Durnford Street further emphasise the military presence. In 1850 a great number of ships were laid up in the Hamoaze, covered with wooden roofs to protect them from the weather, stripped of rigging, and with nothing standing but their lower masts. Over recent years there have of course been several naval vessels kept in moth balls in the Sound in a similar way.

During the Napoleonic wars over 4,000 men were employed to service the fleet at Devonport Dockyards. By 1850 "to satisfy the loud cry which has lately been raised for the reduction of taxes and national expenditure", there were only 1600 shipwrights, caulkers, joiners, smiths, sawyers, rope makers, painters, riggers, sail makers and labourers to keep the peacetime fleet efficiently serviced.

To the east of the Hoe, Catwater Harbour, where the River Plym meets the Sound, could safely shelter 1000 ships, although the great gales of 1824 and 1828 resulted in a total of 35 being driven onto the rocks.

Halfway through the century the Port of Plymouth was thriving. New building at the Gun-Wharf, The Royal William Victualling Yard and Government Steam yard had improved them, and the Steam Floating Bridge, a ponderous vessel, crossed to and from Torpoint and could carry stage coaches without the need to unhorse or for the coachmen and guards needing to alight. There was an extensive coastal trade with steam ships sailing once or twice a week with goods and passengers to London, Southampton, Portsmouth, Guernsey, Jersey, Dublin, Cork etc. Over 4,100 ships entered the port in 1848 carrying around 400,000 tons of cargo. Valuable exports of copper and lead ores, manganese, granite, limestone, clay and fish left through the port daily.

Plymouth had about eighty fishing vessels, sixty of them trawlers and the rest smaller vessels. In the mackerel season there were many boats coming to the area from elsewhere to fish, often between 200 and 300. Turbot, sole, brill, cod, hake and mullet were caught, and salmon, trout and plaice were taken from the Tamar, and all were sold in the local market and sent fresh by train to London, Bath, Bristol, and Manchester. Nowadays the stocks of mackerel have been so depleted by overfishing that they are generally not available whilst in the first twelve days in March 1850 nearly 400 tons left for markets by rail.

Between 1825 and 1850 there was considerable new building in the three towns worthy of comment. As might be predicted this included new churches and schools in each. The state of Plymouth nevertheless included insanitary courts and crowded houses. In 1849 a new borough prison was built, a water supply from Dartmoor replaced the various fountains, and the small reservoir at the head of Old Town Street, a Gas Works was built at Coxside in 1845 and The Exchange Subscription Reading and News Room was established in 1849. Other improvements were the widening of Whimple Street and building an elegant new Post Office here, Charles Chapel in Tavistock Place, Christ Church in Oxford Street, Trinity Church in Southside Street, and Portland Chapel were all built in this short span. In 1834 offices of a befitting handsome nature were built for the branch Bank of England which transferred their premises from Exeter. The increase in the number of schools, growth of charitable institutions and number of societies that were nurtured suggest a thriving community.

Stonehouse, which had benefited from the development of Mill Bay, Sutton Pool, and Hamoaze consolidated its separate indentity by building a large and handsome town hall with a Ball Room, accommodation for the County Court, and apartments for the Stonehouse Literary and Scientific Institution in 1849/50, in an Italianate style. It was fitting that the Royal Western Yacht Club had its headquarters at Mill Bay. In Durnford Street where the buildings still keep much of their former style, St. Paul's Church was completed in 1831. There were also several nonconformist chapels thriving in the area.

Devonport became a borough in 1824, and such was the delight of those living there that they had a column erected from general subscriptions at a cost

T. Allom. W. Le Petit

ENTRANCE TO THE DOCK YARD, FORE STREET, DEVONPORT.

FISHER, SON & Cº LONDON, 1831.

Drawn on Stone by J. D. Harding, from a Sketch taken on the Spot by Captn. G. R. Sartorius R. N. *Printed by C. Hullmandel.*

MOUNT EDGECUMBE, FROM THE HOE.

looking over the Quarries.

Published by W. Byers Bookseller to H. R. H. Duke of Clarence & S. Saunders Repository for Artists, Devonport.

of £2,750. It is of granite and was intended to have a colossal statue of George IV, who had granted the charter, to top it. Unfortunately the money ran out and only the column was completed to catch the eye from Union Street, and no doubt to remind Plymouth of Devonport's independence. It had the style of a market town with a market in poultry and butter over the shambles, spacious accommodation in the Royal and London Hotels in Fore street with assembly rooms in the former. Several of the seventeen dissenting chapels were built during this time of growth, and St. Michaels Chapel of Ease in Navy Row was built in 1843, St. James in Morice Town in 1849 and St. Paul's in Morice Square was finished during 1850/51.

From the descriptions of the facilities to be found in Devonport ranging from the Sea Baths near Richmond walk where hot, cold, shower, vapour and swimming baths were provided to the Pleasure Fair on Whit Monday, and the Rowing Regatta held in the summer, it is evident that it was just as capable of providing for most of those living there as could the other two towns.

The elegance of those years has been lost and so too has much of the disparity of wealth that was able to maintain it. Each of the parts of modern Plymouth that once ran independently have little reminders of the separate towns they once were.

T. Allom. M. J. Starling.

CITADEL, POOL, QUEEN ANNE'S BATTERY, &c. PLYMOUTH.

FISHER, SON, & Co LONDON. 1830.

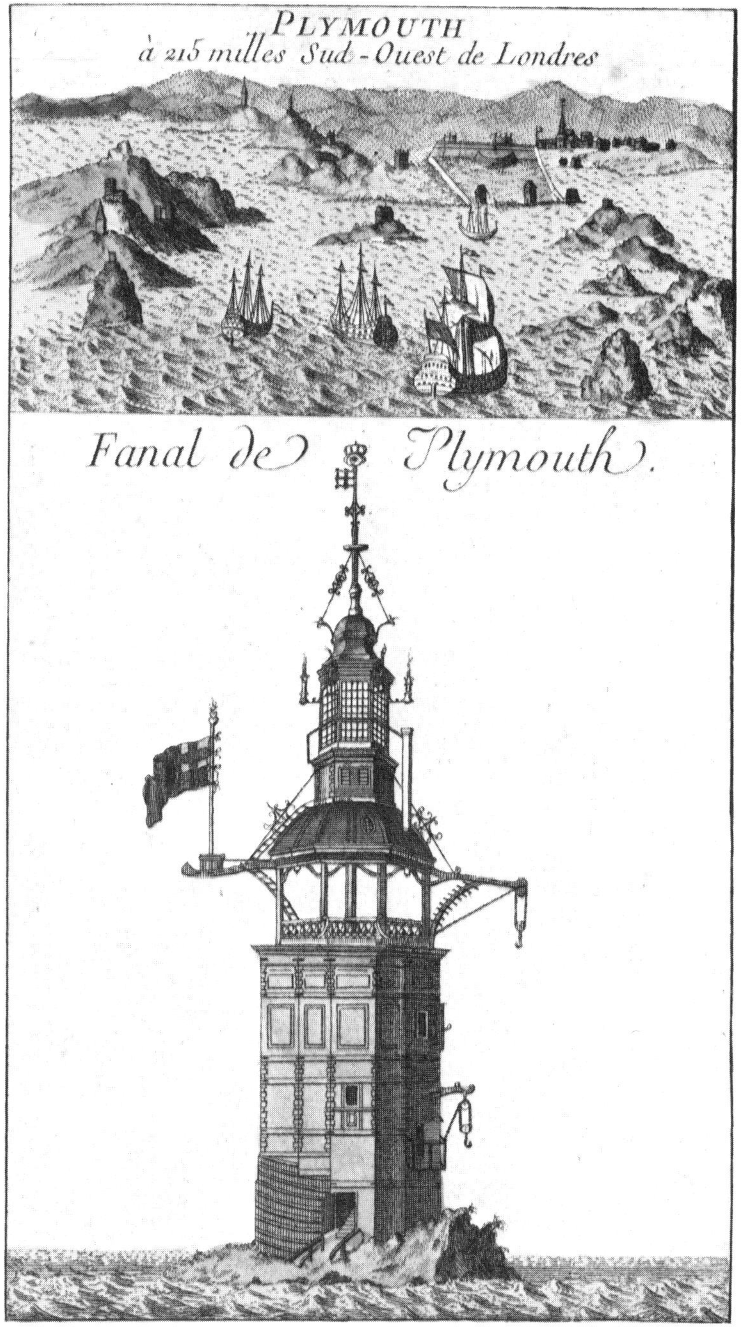
PLYMOUTH
à 215 milles Sud-Ouest de Londres
Fanal de Plymouth.

8. South Devon

by the Reverend John Swete

About the beginning of May 1795, I went with my family to Dawlish wishing to try what good effects a change of air and sea bathing might produce on myself, who from a long confinement, during the whole of one of the unremitting attacks of the rheumatism, had suffered a great relaxation, as well as, on my two youngest children, who in consequence of inoculation had been exceedingly debilitated.

Dawlish was once a fishing hamlet, consisting of a few cots, one or two of which had been fitted up for the occassional reception of an invalid stranger, and on the cliffs and over the Strand edifices of superior tast and higher expense crowd together – I wish I could have added, in some sort of systematical arrangement. About 20 years ago the price of the best lodging house per week was not more, if it was as much, as half a guinea, but so fashionable is Dawlish in the present day, that in the height of the season, not a house of the least consequence is to be hired for less than two guineas per week, and many of them rise to so high a sum as four or five.

The cliffs are here at the Western extremities of the Strand of considerable magnificence bold and perpendicular, not however of a very dense and compact stratum, as is clear from the encroachments which the spray and surge of the sea have made on them, huge fragments being scattered at their foot, and immense masses shaped often into grotesque forms, standing at some distance off in the water which being of a more solid nature here withstood the buffeting of assailing elements.

The view beyond takes in part of the new range of buildings on the shore before which runs the public Mall. Through the hedgerow openings the range of houses conducting to the Strand have a good effect, and the termination of the little valley on the shore is a pleasing circumstance. The curvature of the shore gives the appearance of a bay, but one too extensive to admit of shelter for vessels.

The Grist Mill near the Strand, as singularly situated, and picturesque, seldom fails of attracting the stranger of more than common observation. It is an overshot mill, as is the case with all in these parts, and the stream falling over a ledge of gravel ere it comes to the wheel, forms a little cascade which gives somewhat of a romantic air to the scene. The stream that acts on it is diverted from the little river that runs from Ashcombe down the narrow valley of Dawlish pursuing its course, placid clear through its deep and rugged channel.

From the Strand to the Church is about the distance of a mile, and though there is now some intervening space of fields and gardens, yet if the rage for building continues to increase in a few years, the one will be to the other not only "non longo proscimus intervallo" but altogether connected with it. On entering the churchyard one is struck with the picturesque scenery, a noble Gothic pile surrounded by elms of considerable size. I have seldom met with a handsomer front than on the Southern aspect.

The vicarage house stands enclosed by its gardens and boasts a naturalisation as it were of exotics which elsewhere require the fostering aid of art.

At this comparatively retired watering place, I took up my abode for six weeks. On May 29th I left Dawlish, and having passed through the lower village of Holcombe passed Gorway Cross, by a declevity of a mile, I approached the town of East Teignmouth, having in full prospect its picturesque scenery, its harbour a wide expanse of sea and the opening of Torbay.

On the sands, near the commencement of the rapidly ascending cliffs, I sketched the Church of East Teignmouth, and some of its new buildings, which seem to brave the fury of the waves, though they have encroached on the sands and have raised their foundations on the walls of a house which at some past time had been demolished by the tide.

Beyond them is perceived the entrance of the port and the singular promontory of the Nase extending itself from the village of Shaldon.

Taking my way now by the side of a most charming terrace walk, which in a line parallel to the Strand, extends from the easternmost point of the Den, to the furthermost margin of its sod on the West, I passed by a new fortress which has been within the last year raised on the site of the ancient one that had fallen to decay. On its rampart are mounted four cannon, which if they are not destined to contribute to the defence of the town, may, by their roar on gala days serve to express the loyalty and exultation of its inhabitants.

Arriving at the point opposite Shaldon I hailed the ferry boat, which having reached the Strand, just as a sloop, and two mast fishing boats were working their way up the gut of the harbour, I detained

Duncan, Sculp.

THE BRIDGE FROM THE NESS.

Published by W. T. Strutt & Son, Exeter & Teignmouth.

Printed by Fisher, London.

apprehensive that one of my horses, a young one that had never been in a boat might be terrified at the motion of the vessels, and the shifting of their sails.

The wind blowing along from the west, and full in their teeth, and the tide being about half flow, they had no little difficulty in entering the harbour, in this short passage, not above two or three gun shots long, they were obliged to tack 3 times, and I was a good deal amused by the dexterity of the seamen, and the beautiful appearance of the vessels, as they scudded along gunnels to, when they caught a side breeze.

Dawlish and Teignmouth are as popular with holidaymakers today as they were at the beginning of the nineteenth century. At that time Teignmouth was a thriving port through which passed pipe and potters' clay dug up in the neighbouring parish of Kingsteignton. In 1820 George Templer had completed the new quay for this trade, as well as for transporting granite used in building throughout the country. For centuries boat building was important, but now this has stopped, although there are more pleasure craft than ever before. In recent years the export of clays and the use of the port have increased, and proposals for development below the magnificent bridge with its thirty-four arches, built in 1826, suggest even more riverside activity.

The bridge was an elegant testimony to the Victorian engineer, but equally utilitarian for the town was the new reservoir and provision of gas around 1836.

At the start of the century when East and West Teignmouth were separated by little more than a brook there were 2,000 villagers, but by 1850 when they remained separate in name only there were 4,400. The Den provides the town with some dignity and a pleasant open space, beloved by small boys and dogs alike. There are some commendable old streets in the town, although perhaps Shaldon keeps a cosier nineteenth century feeling than Teignmouth whose immediate attractions are not enhanced by the new roads that bypass the quainter and more ancient parts. A ferry still runs from Teignmouth but the "Naze" is now called The Ness.

Dawlish centre has been kept within the limits of the valley in which it first developed and its growth has been influenced by the enclosing hills which rise behind providing a cosiness which belies the amount of recent development. The South Devon railway was unfortunately built across the lower end of the valley on a viaduct designed by Brunel, and completed in 1846. This rather detracts from the view although there is easy access beneath it to the beach. By 1809 much of the building facing onto the lawn had been completed, as had the straightening of the river that splashes over small water falls as it flows through it. The old mill wheel is now rather derelict but the neat houses and villas are distinctively trim and attractive. The building to the south of the Church about the lawn, completed by 1850, gives the whole town a charm and relaxed style. Sadly only the red sandstone tower remains from the old Church of St. Michael – now St. Gregory – which was rebuilt in 1824/5. The buildings of Stonelands and Luscombe Castle built around 1800 by Nash working with Repton who landscaped their grounds, just at the edge of the town, are perhaps symbolic of the wealth and elegance of those times.

Both towns were said to have good shops in the early part of the century and whatever the alterations this is still so. The coastal scenery is stunningly unchanged, and the rocks at Dawlish seen by Swete were fittingly called the Parson and Clerk rocks. By 1850 each of the towns had four nonconformist chapels and there were of course improved schools.

In 1794 Swete visited Torquay which he describes as little more than expanding villages.

DAWLISH

The Beach, Dawlish, South Devon.

The Strand, Dawlish, South Devon.

Dawlish. South Devon (from the heights)

Piermont Place, Dawlish, Devon.

H. Haseler, Delt.   D. Havell, Sculpt.

HARBOUR AND VIEW OF TORQUAY. FROM THE WEST.

Published, Novr 1st 1818, by J. Wallis, Marine Library, Sidmouth.

TORQUAY.

FROM THE PIER HEAD.

Drawn from nature & on Stone and Published by Geo. Rowe

Mount Radford Exeter.

Printed by Engelmann & Co.

Immediately behind the houses on the Quay, the ground ascends in the most rapid manner. In many parts the rock appears with a smooth and perpendicular surface evidently hewn from the original slope, to afford an area for the buildings. A greater variety of pleasing and romantic scenery will rarely be met with – rocks, woods, houses, a villa and the sea, are intermingled in the happiest manner, altogether forming a landscape of uncommon beauty. The vessels also with their masts and rigging peeping from among the trees, are pleasing objects, and not only contribute to enhance the scenery, but point out the situation of the quays.

Tor Abbey from the pier rises into importance, its groves are more discriminated and the hills behind with the cottages of the village of Chilson have the most rural effect. At the ebb or spring tides, these level sands at Torquay, are left bare and uncovered for a considerable distance. They are firm and of a fine nature.

From the southern most end of the houses a pathway leads over the cliffs, which rise in a progressive series, and from the north barrier of the Bay, at near a mile distance, their perpendicular height is from two to three hundred feet and there, where the waters begin to expand I observed a vast chasm between the mainland and an immense mass of rocks, which seemed to have owed its separation to some violent convulsion of nature, more inland I perceived deep fissures, which exclusive of their horizontal direction, have a strong resemblance to the zig zag rents of ruinous castles. From this fearful chasm, which I ventured not too near to approach, a number of trees, chiefly Ash, had grown to considerable size.

Returning to the little footway behind the Quay I followed it, as it winded up a dell among the rocks. An old dilapidated lime kiln here presented itself, the rock above it from whence the stones had been dug, for the whole stratum of the country is marble, showed itself with a broad front, and as it spread itself onwards on both sides it sweetly displayed its rude and natural crags intermingling with a variety of underwood among which the sorbus was conspicuously beautiful contrasting its silvery foliage with the dark green tints that surrounded it.

At the entrance of this little path from a field at the eastern end of the village a very pleasing view of Torwood House offered itself. A charming rich vale winded down the bottom towards the sea, on one side secured from its blasts by the rocky hill where the ruinous lime kiln lay, and on the other skirted by a continued line of branching oaks. Through these the road ran that conducted me to the house, which was not quite half a mile distant from the Quay.

From the fine grove behind Torwood House I passed through an avenue of handsome oaks, the top branches of which I was sorry to see were on the decay, seemingly from old age, and soon after I skirted the field, on the north side of which a rock of marble, overhung by a wood is the cavern, known by the name of "Kents hole". This I could not at present visit, as I had no candles. I moved on to the farm of Hilson, where I was gratified with the sight of objects equally curious, and under the influence of a genial sunbeam infinitely more agreeable.

Turning northward, on the verge of a wild down, I soon reached Ansty Cove, where the mountainous cliffs frown in majestic grandeur, high towering over the waters that incessant lash their sides. From thence I rode on over their green sward summits, till at once arriving at a precipice my eye glanced downward over the scattered village of Babbicombe. This is a sort of scenery that seldom occurs on our coast but it is not merely uncommon, it is picturesque and romantic. An immense hill is beheld descending towards a bay formed by projecting headlands on the north and south, in general the descent is rapid. There are spots however about midway down where the ground shelves away gradually, and sometimes assumes the form of a level, of every one of these spots advantage hath been taken, cottages appear, with their little gardens not infrequently surrounded by trees. At the first entrance of this village my attention was arrested by a series of enormous rocks, that overshadowed it on the South.

By degrees, leading my horse, I threaded, as it were, all the intricacies of the declevity, charmed at almost every step with some new beauty either in the situation of a cottage, or the prospect, and at length got to the bottom.

Here were some large and handsome trees, and the dilapidated walls of a house were immediately before me, and contiguous there to a beach which was full of life and bustle. A number of fishing smacks were just come to their moorings, and the side of a projecting point of rock that lay nearly in the centre of the little bay, was a barge from Topsham, receiving her cargo of limestone.

After a good lounge in this delightful spot I regained the summit. I remounted with no small degree of satisfaction, and from the northern point took a last look of this uncommonly situated village. As the cottages all hung, as it were, on the opposite slope, from hence they were beheld in all their different sites, tier above tier, the chimneys of some (if the wind served) fumigating the windows of others.

From thence, a small plain, unfenced from a continuous line of precipice, and a short lane brought me to Marychurch. The church, reputed the oldest in the County I discovered on the north side of the

Drawn by T. H. Williams.

Engraved by T. Higham.

BABICOMBE,

NEAR TORQUAY, DEVON.

Nave, within the edifice, two circular arches, which are different from all the rest, even from those two which are opposite and assist in the support of the same part of the roof. This is a singular circumstance but is hardly of sufficient force to establish the tradition of its Saxon or Norman origin.

Riding through the village, I again turned down a miry lane towards the sea. This soon brought me to the cliffs whence to the south I had a view of Babbicombe Bay, and northward of the town of Teignmouth, Dawlish and Exmouth. Immediately below lay Petit loe cove, into which by a steep winding path, formed out of a stratum of purple schists, I descended to the spot from whence those beautiful and newly discovered marbles have been drawn. The field of the marble is of several tints, grey or reddish, charged with a profusion of darker coloured spots.

From this place . . . at the end of a woody hedgerow where the way suddenly turns, a grand quarry of marble rocks rises steep crowned on its high summit by rich oaks, and underwood. To the right of this ascends boldly the mountainous hill which backs the western part of Torquay, whose summit and side towards the sea hath been enriched by Mr. Cary's plantations. In the mid scene, is just descried the tops of rows of houses in the meadow – those that block it up towards the bay, a rocky promentory beyond with a petty fortification on its top, a catch of the bay itself, and the range of hills that rising above the town of Brixham extended themselves to Berry Head.

Having now made my retour to Torquay, and having scrutinised it with a picturesque eye, I shall now turn to Tor Abbey. From Torquay the proper road to the house and grounds passes by Tor Church, but there is a footpath, which by a steep and rugged ascent rises from the building of the western part of the cove, and is carried on the elevated ridge of an immense cliff of marble, and protected only from the precipice, by a stunted fence of brushwood.

From hence in my way to Torr Abbey I passed into inclosure, part of which lay in front of the house. Here is a prospect of the range of cliffs, that rises as a boundary to the bay on the north. The more distant ones bare and rugged their sides craggy and their summits irregularly pointed. Beneath these, thrusting itself forward into the water appears the little sodded fortress with its pole. The rounded hill comes in view with a peculiar and striking contrast shelving away rapidly to the Quay, a few of the houses of which are discerned with the vessels moored before them.

Between the trunks of a row of noble oaks whose side and upper branches formed a sylvan arch, I had a most pleasing view of the front of Tor Abbey House with its wings and the old gateway.

The site of the Abbey being low, and the ground rising between it and the water, to obviate this obstruction of the most important part of the prospect, the new building is of the more than common elevation. There is an ascent to the lower rooms, which I apprehend are of little consequence, by a flight of steps and the suite of apartments occupied by the family are those on the first floor. I sat an hour with Mr. Cary, who had returned from Bath a few days before I quitted Torquay, in one of the front rooms of this storey, and I think I never saw from any apartment a more delicious prospect. How enchanting to command from ones window, as is frequently the case, the grand fleet of Great Britain here riding at anchor, making its entrance into the Bay in majestic state, or taking its departure from it.

The remains of the chapel and barn are in evidence and testify not only to the strength towers and battlements, and the barn is capacious enough to stow an immense quantity of corn, perhaps equal to the annual consumption of the monastry. According to the tradition of the country this barn at one time served as a repository for other matters than the produce of the harvest. A chaff cutter therein employed told me "that it was once nearly filled with the dead bodies of Spaniards, who, having landed with an intent of plundering the Abbey, were kept on shore by means of an English fleet that unexpectedly entered the Bay, and flying for refuge to this Barn were there shut up and starved to death."

How much of marvellous exaggeration may have contributed to the embellishment of the savage story I cannot ascertain, but it appears that the place had suffered some hostile attack, from some cannon ball having been found lodged in the garden wall which intervened between the Abbey and the Sea.

Having reached the end of the last avenue at Tor Abbey, southward I proceeded on the Paignton Road as far as the skirts of the village of Chilsum. I then turned quick to the right, ascending a little hill, I passed through a mean looking gateway and at once had in view before me Cockington House and Church on the rising part of the hill contiguous to the gardens of the Mansion, this being surrounded by old walls and trees had rather a picturesque look.

From hence I regained the lane, which brought me to the Newton – Dartmouth roads. This after half a mile I crossed turning down a steep lane to the right, and having passed through part of Compton Village I arrived at the Castle. The front towards the north had a great deal of magnificence, and its towers, gateway and machicolations shewed the remains of strength. The barns and cow houses con-

Drawn by R. Brown. Esqr Arch^{t} — Engraved by H. Willis

COCKINGTON COURT, DEVON.

THE SEAT OF THE REV^{D} ROGER MALLOCK, TO WHOM THIS PLATE IS MOST RESPECTFULLY INSCRIBED BY THE PROPRIETORS.

London Published by R. Jennings & W. Chaplin. 62. Cheapside.

tinguous, though excellent in their kind, detract from its picturesque appearance.

The eastern end of the building in its roof and windows hath received some modern alterations being fitted up for the reception of a farmer who rents the Estate. The other parts, though in a state of dilapidation retain the castellated form they wore during the time of its ancient possessors.

In 1800 the traveller passing through Torbay must have enjoyed one of the most outstandingly beautiful sights that has ever been lost. Torquay was little more than a fishing village which with remarkable speed grew to 9,000 fifty years later and in doing so merged with the village of Torre, whilst St. Mary Church became a suburb. At the turn of the century however the growth, at first encouraged by the presence of the Fleet and afterwards by the soft climate and sheltered conditions, had scarcely begun. Even at the half century the bay must still have looked only sparcely inhabited so that blue sea and skies, fine sandy beaches, precipitous cliffs and gently rolling hills behind, well tree'd and equally well cultivated were hardly touched by intrusive building.

Things have changed, and almost the whole of the bay is built up, the hills and craggy valley rocks have often been lost amongst the houses although the quality of Torbay has still managed to remain in a superior vein. Over 113,000 people now crowd the area and those separate villages seen by Swete give their names to suburban parts of Torquay and Paignton. The Ilsham Valley which is part of St. Mary Church Parish is starred with well-to-do houses and hotels, whilst Kents Cavern has from 1825 increasingly attracted sightseers. For a small sum it is possible to take a short walk in the caves which have been carefully lit so that one may enjoy the stalagmites and stalactites, often with mineral colouring green, red or greyish blue, and see some of the prehistoric animal remains on show in the souvenir shop.

Many of the early Victorian villas and terraces serve as hotels or guest houses, and Tor Abbey and its gardens open as a museum. The elms and oaks have been lost, but other trees have been planted in its grounds. The house is a local museum and the Spanish barn of the thirteenth century stands close by. There is a cannon-ball taken from the Barn's wall in the museum.

There remain many pleasant places and possibly Cockington ranks amongst the most notable. The village is preserved in a combe set back from Livermead Sands and the ancient parish church stands close to Cockington Court, which is owned by the Borough.

Compton Castle, to the north of Torquay, was already in a dilapidated state in 1850, but miraculously it has survived the intervening years and recently been well restored by the late Commander Gilbert, a descendant of one of the earliest owners, the Elizabethan explorer who discovered the Gilbert and Ellis Islands. This ancient castellated manor, unique in Devon, is opened by the National Trust to the public.

On the 18th of June taking leave of Torquay for a few days, after a delightful ride, at one time on the hills commanding the Bay, and at another on its sands which at low water are firm and hard, I entered the town of Paignton, I now paid a visit to the remains of the Episcopal Palace, and had the satisfaction of having my curiosity amply repaid. Near the western end of the Church, yet standing, the gateway that led into the Palace. This however seems never to have been of consequence. The principal buildings lay south east of this and are boundaries on these points of the churchyard.

The sands lie not more than a field or two from the Church and at ebb of tide offer to the sight as fine a beach as can be imagined.

Paignton cannot be said to have the same elegance as Torquay. It started to develop rather later although it had doubled its population by 1850 to 1575. Its attractive sands like those of Torquay entice the holidaymakers and windsurfers, and the front has a neat lawn and cafe, with a terrace of Victorian houses which are now exclusively hotels behind it. Like Torquay it is an amiable place, although with possibly less variety of shops. In the summer a steam train hisses its way to Kingswear and back in an authentically Victorian way.

The town stretches up the hill to the north of the old village which was built back from the sea. Here the remains of the Bishop's Palace can be found, tucked away at the rear of St. John's churchyard, undisturbed but not enhanced by some new development close by. The shops and houses near the Church appear to be mid Victorian, whilst nearby Kirkham house, a stone and slate property dating from the medieval times and possibly connected with the Bishops Palace, has recently been restored and opened by the Department of the Environment to the public. This small area is attractive in its scale and age and in Mill Street the ancient clink is divided into two cells, and was doubtless in use well before 1800.

Engraved by John Smith from a Drawing by G. Shepherd after a Sketch by S. Prout. for the Beauties of England & Wales.

COMPTON CASTLE,
Devonshire.

London: Published by Verner, Hood & Sharpe, Poultry, Octr. 1. 1807.

Drawn by T. H. Williams.

Engraved by J. Eke

VIEW FROM THE PARAPET OF THE PUBLIC ROOMS, TEIGNMOUTH, DEVON.

London. Published by Robert Jennings, 62, Cheapside, June 1, 1830.

Haseler. Del.t D. Havell. Sculp.t

GORES LIBRARY, ON THE BEACH, DAWLISH.

Published by J. Wallis, Marine Library, Sidmouth.

H. Haseler. Del.t D. Havell. Sculp.t

VIEW OF THE PARSON AND CLERK, FROM DAWLISH.

The red soils behind Paignton were once renowned for their orchards, and cider was shipped in small vessels to London, returning with coal. They also produced the locally renowned large Paignton cabbages, which like cider are less in evidence now than a hundred years ago.

Leaving the shore I ascended a small eminence, the road crossing a narrow headland which cut off all communication with the sands on the other side, this having passed I dipped again to another beach, from whence there was a pleasing opening by a narrow vale to the inner country. I now quitted the sea coast altogether, rising towards the uplands, and having rode through the village of Gorington soon after joined at the turnpike gate, the Newton, Dartmouth and Brixham roads. This last I proceeded on, with the view of seeing Lupton the seat of Sir Frances Buller.

A ride of a quarter of a mile brought me to Lupton, through newly planted grounds rising high and quick from the road to the right, pleasantly through a most luxuriant shrubbery, well sheltered by the forest trees at their backs and a continuance of the hill. From this avenue, dispensing gales of fragrance from a variety of flowering shrubs, I entered a lawn which led immediately to the house.

Lupton lies in the parish of Brixham. Turning westward from the house I rode up a rural valley, skirted by the wood and beaches.

PAIGNTON.

Drawn by E. Duncan

Engraved by E. Finden.

BRIXHAM.

London Published for the Proprietors by Geo Virtue, 26, Ivy Lane

T. Allom. F. J. Havill.

DARTMOUTH.

FISHER, SON, & Cº LONDON. 1837.

Lupton had been rebuilt by Charles Hayne and sold to Sir Francis Butler in 1788. Its freshly planted oaks and other hardwood trees now embellish the rolling hills which surround the House now used as a School, in rich maturity. Brixham has since the earliest times been divided between Upper and Lower Brixham, or perhaps more descriptively, Fish-town centred on the quay with terraces tumbling down an attractive valley to it, with Cow-town on the hills above. Pictures of Brixham around 1830 show a jumble of terraces with smoking chimneys and innumerable boats sailing to and fro. Its population doubled in fifty years to over 7,000, and most were in some way dependent upon the fishing fleet, the largest it was claimed, in England. There were more than 270 sail of vessels, amounting to 20,000 tons and employing 1600 seamen.

Today Brixham is the premier fishing port in Devon taking 47% of the value of all fish caught, with the Dart and Salcombe fleets landing the most crabs and lobsters. About 8,800 tonnes of fish were landed here in 1981, and between 300 and 400 people are employed. Already the mackerel stock has been decimated and experiments using electrodes to increase flat fish catches promise further depletion which in the end could destroy Brixham's prosperity.

The school was modernised in 1820, and often enough the school register records the departure of children with the fishing fleet. With the population increase came a District Church at Lower Brixham in 1820, a Baptist Chapel in 1801, a Wesleyan Chapel in 1816, and an Independent Chapel in 1843.

The Brixham fishing boats are moored by the old pier, built in 1804, within the inner harbour, close to the statue of William, Prince of Orange who landed here on 5th November 1688. To relieve the crowded harbour and provide for all the numerous fishing vessels an outer breakwater was started in 1845, but not completed until the beginning of this century.

The two fortresses that were built on Berry Head during the Napoleonic Wars are in good repair. The one closest to the National Trust Car Park was the second to be built, and has a diminutive lighthouse on it, and a coastguards station. A lively idea of its defences has been fostered by putting some restored cannon there. In 1850 a coastguard station was manned at Queens Quay and another on Man Sands, but the modern one has views on a clear day to Portland in the East and along the South Hams coast to Plymouth in the West.

About 1840 iron ore was discovered and mined. It was exported for some years from the Brixham Quays to Wales, and the yellow ochre which was found with the ore has until recently been used for the manufacture of paint.

C Stanfield R.A. J.B. Allen sc.

DARTMOUTH.

I now, after a most delightful walk, for as soon as the declevity of the hill became any way rapid I dismounted from my horse, having had the refreshing breezes of the Ocean playing on my face the whole way, entered Kingswear, and on arriving at the place of embarkation for Dartmouth, I found the boat engaged by a full complement of passengers and horses, so that I was under the necessity of taking a lounge till its return. In the course of which strolling into a yard near the boathouse I observed the Church in a picturesque point, forming with the Inn and other houses in the street near the ferry, no unpleasing assemblage of objects.

The tide flowing with a high and unruffled wave I was soon put ashore on the landing place and that without difficulty. On gaining the Inn, and being recognised by the landlady Mrs. Pentecost, a flaunting Dame and fair – in an authoritative tone she bade the waiter usher me to the Apollo. This was a large front sitting room pleasantly commanding the Quay and River.

After dinner which was not over sumptuous or excessive I proceeded from Cromwells tower, instead of descending to the shore as I had formerly when I visited the castles on the cliffs, I now turned to the right, by some rope walks, and having mastered a long and rugged hill, after a ride of two miles with no object of consequence in view but the sea, I reached the village of Stoke Fleming, so named from a Flemish nobleman who possessed it in King Johns time.

Two ferries take vehicles across the Dart between Kingswear and Dartmouth and maintain the old tradition. No longer is there a muddy beach to negotiate, because in the late nineteenth century the modern quays were formed by filling in the edge of the river and providing a firm quayside and central pool. Above St. Saviours Church and the Elizabethan houses that jostle along the narrow roads around Bayards Cove, terraces of houses with communicating alleys and steps climb the hills, and looking majestically towards the open sea by Old Mill Creek is the Royal Naval College, designed by Sir Aston Webb and built between 1902-1904.

The steep wooded sides of the Dart Valley create an unparalleled setting for a pleasant holiday town and yatching centre. The castles of Kingswear and Dartmouth like the romantic ruins of the one at Salcombe are features of interest.

The population of Dartmouth doubled to 5000 or thereabouts in 1850, although the small village of Kingswear with 250 inhabitants had grown relatively little. Now the population of Dartmouth is only 6,000 and the livelihood of people who live here and at Kingswear and Salcombe is largely bound up with agriculture and fishing, although over 300,000 holidaymakers come to this part of the coast each year.

A mile, after having dipped down a very steep hill, brought me to the village of Blackpool, a place which offered itself to the notice of the French Admiral de Castle on account of its conveniency for landing his troops and from whence it is more than probable he marched to the attack he made on Dartmouth in the reign of Henry IV in which he not only failed, but was himself taken prisoner. With other villages in the vicinity Blackpool was plundered and set afire by the French, it now possesses but a few houses scattered on the sides of the hills and on the beach.

I continued on then for near two miles when I again made a descent on the sands of Slapton which had taken their commencement. I now had before me one of the most singular appearances I had ever met with. I rode on a ridge of sand having on my left the Sea, and on my right a lake of fresh water, the one is separated from the other only by this bank of sand which is not above the width of two common gunshots, and it is a cause for admiration, how so inconsiderable a barrier should be able to withstand the furious dashings of a tempestuous sea on the one hand, and the weight of water of the lake on the other, which is about three miles long and in some parts a quarter mile broad.

I learnt that it had once such an opening made, as to let out the major part of its own water, and admit those of the sea, an event that was fatal to the fish that were within it. This aperture however was soon again closed by the shifting sands and there is now no appearance of the breach that had once been made. The first part of the lake or lea as it is called, at this season of the year, mid summer, was in a manner covered over by a thick crop of sedgy reeds.

At the termination of this sedgy part of the Lea there is a bridge, of two or three arches over the water which is here much contracted, forming a communiction with the village of Slapton, that lies about half a mile inland. At this place on the sands is seen a house and some outbuildings called Slapton cellars. I was told, by a fisherman that it abounded in Pike, Perch, Roach and Eels.

The village of Tarcross though inconsiderable, consisting chiefly

Drawn by T. M. Baynes. Engraved by W. Deeble.

WARFLEET BAY, NEAR DARTMOUTH.

DEVONSHIRE.

London Published by R. Jennings & W. Chaplin, 62 Cheapside. 1830.

of but one range of small houses, is yet extremely neat, and being built near the Lea, hath a very pleasing appearance. Several of the cottages are hired during the summer months, by families in the neighbouring towns, and most of them have from their windows views of the sea and of the lake.

Here I had intended to have taken up my quarters for the night but having two or three hours of day yet before me I resolved to push forward to Salcombe.

The coastline between Brixham and Plymouth is probably as attractive as can be found anywhere, with cliffs that rise in rugged fashion often up to 400 feet above the sea breaking on rocks below, divided by the estuaries of the Dart, Avon, Erme and Yealm, and Salcombe Harbour. The extensive beaches of Bantham, Thurlestone and Slapton are the bonus sought by holidaymakers. Within the wide spaces of the South Hams there are only 67,000 people, and most of them live at Kingsbridge, Dartmouth, Totnes and Ivybridge, and only the latter has mushroomed enormously since 1850.

In 1850 Stoke Fleming had over 700 people living there with a new vicarage built in 1834 and a National school built in 1843. The village has become enlarged in recent times and has a few old buildings in the centre. It is within easy reach of the nearby Blackpool sands, which are at the entrance of a cove with the dark greenish cliffs on either side. Slapton Sands, no more than a mile or so further on can scarcely have changed at all, and is now principally known for the fresh water lake, Slapton Ley, which is a nature reserve. The Slapton Field centre attracts students to study the abundant plant and animal life of the lake and its marshes. In 1850 the size of Slapton was similar to Stoke Fleming, and like it has grown particularly on the hills about. It is especially attractive close to the ancient church where nearby stone and thatched cottages flank narrow roads. The American Memorial which records thanks to the people who lived in the area for their sacrifice in leaving their homes to allow military training in the area prior to the D Day landings in June 1944 stands on the site of Slapton cellars.

Torcross is a neat row of houses with a hotel and village shop which caters for holidaymakers. Stokenham was the largest of the villages in the area, about twice the size of Slapton, in 1850, and is still so. The parish church, St. Michaels and All Angels, stands boldly on a hill on the edge of the village and nearby are a number of good stone and thatch cottages, as well as considerably greater numbers of modern bungalows and houses.

Not long however had I journeyed ere I reached a stone directing Post, which being of a pentagonal figure, had a letter on each compartment pointing to an opposite lane. Here observing two S'ess contiguous to each other, I found myself at a loss which road to take, I therefore, after a little hesitating pursued that which was most considerable, but looking after I had rode about a furlong, I discovered a man following me. This discovery proved fortunate, for from him I learnt I was making for Start Point, instead of Salcombe, a circumstance that evinces how necessary it is for directing posts to be correct and particular.

Start Point lay about a mile southward of me and comprising a considerable Barton is possessed by Mr. Bastard of Kitley.

At length after having mastered many a hill and descended as often into the vales, I came in view of a creek belonging to Salcombe water. Here was a pleasantly situated village called Waterhead through which the road ran.

The views were very pleasing, and at one point in particular, where I had a command of the esturary up to the town of Kingsbridge, they were extremely fine. I now made a little circuit round the walls of the parsonage house of Portlemouth. The church lay more southward approaching Praul point, the most southerly spot in the County, the situation was beautiful, and building of an antique cast, embosomed among venerable elms which resounded with cawings of Rooks, was uncommonly rural and picturesque.

From this sequestered spot, I passed on to the shore, descending from the low rocky cliffs by means of a little trackway hewn out for the convenience of travellers, who by a ferry boat pass over the water to Salcombe. To the left where was the entrance to the harbour, on a rock appeared the ruins of an old castle. This edifice which seemed much delapidated seemed to occupy the whole rock.

The little town of Salcombe seated at the foot of a considerable hill, lay before me. There was a most rural admixture of trees with houses, which in one part rose above each other on the steep sides of the hill, as the town of Dartmouth, in a most picturesque manner.

To my enquiries about an Inn, one of the persons in the boat, offered me his home. It seems that there were two public houses in the place, rivals to one another, and the landlord of one of them perceiving strangers on the opposite bank, by joining the boatman thought it was a fair occasion for securing them to himself – it answered his purpose, and I soon found myself lodged in a decent house called the Kings Arms.

The next morning I reconnoitred the place and in the midst of it

Salcombe. Devon.

discovered the ruins of a building which appeared to have been, in its better day a chapel. Down the street was an outlet to the water, presenting a prospect of it, as far as the creek at Watershed, and in the mid most opening in on the left, pointing out the wavy way to the town of Kingsbridge.

After breakfast I proceeded on to Molt, a summer villa of Mr. Strode of Peamore. From the windows of which between Bolt Head a high craggy promontory on the right, and Peartree point on the most Southern part of the Country, is beheld the entrance from the channel to the haven of Salcombe and Kingsbridge. There is a grandeur in the stupendous natural avenue which is indescribably fine, but which is heightened to an uncommon degree when through its vast rugged sides.

Bolt Head gradually rising towards the inner country, and forming a huge barrier to the waters to the west presents a wild scenery of rock and furzeland, dotted sparingly with enclosures. To the left of the haven's mouth, the grounds rise also high and rough featured, till they reach the cultivated environs of the village of Portlemouth, which in a succession of farms, surrounded by woods, from amongst which the houses frequently appear, descends from near the summit of an eminence, to the rocks on the waters edge.

From Marlborrow, where I observed no entrenchments or tumuli from whence it might be supposed to have derived its appellation, I rode on the road leading to Kingsbridge for three miles, I then turned from it to the left for Modbury gathering my information from one of the best directing posts I ever saw.

Waterhead has an enviable situation at the head of a creek in this beautiful and remote part of the County which like similar nearby spots attract retired folk. Portlemouth (East) is small enough and has such stupendous views of the Salcombe Estuary and Coast including the cliffs between Prawle Point and Bolt Head that time might have forgotten this southerly outpost of the County.

Salcombe is a small and attractive town and has only grown by a thousand since 1850 when 1500 lived there. The belief at this time was that it was the warmest place on the south west coast, as oranges, lemons, and American aloes bloomed in the open in the pleasure grounds of two fine mansions – Woodville (now Woodcot) and Moult. At this time the haven could shelter up to 200 ships, and vessels of 200 tons would go up to Kingsbridge. Sometimes mail bags were landed here and coal, culm, groceries and foreign fruit came ashore at the port, whilst there were exports of corn, flour, malt and cider.

The more recent attraction of Slapton Sands for holidaymakers and the numerous sailing boats add a sparkle to an attractive town. There is a small passenger ferry that crosses the estuary between Salcombe and East Portlemouth throughout the year manned by a bearded sailor in the most traditional way. In 1801 the old chapel was rebuilt mainly at the expense of John Yates of Woodville, but it was later found to be too small and a new district church, Holy Trinity was built with public subscriptions and grants in 1843, six years before the Wesleyan Chapel. A National school was completed in 1849, whilst the Kings Arms has continued to satisfy the needs of thirsty travellers to the present day. The narrow streets and slate hung buildings in the lower and oldest part of the town embody the spirit of this traditional fishing village.

A few houses and a local shop huddle close to the windswept Malborough Church, and the few ancient properties close to it are supplemented by too many new ones, although modest in number when compared to the development at East and West Charlton across the estuary. Kingsbridge with a modest population of 2,500 was most salubrious and clean, just as it is today. The buildings of Dodbrooke, are terraced down hill to the quay where the estuary brings the smell of the sea and sight of pleasure boats to this market town. It was in 1804 that a barracks for 600 soldiers was built as part of the war efforts, but shortly after dismantled.

Kingbridge's main shopping street rises up above the quay in a gentle curve and the motorist sent up the one way street sees an attractive array of shops and slate hung buildings. The shambles, which is the old Market Hall rebuilt in 1796 as an arcade over the pavement, the curious clock tower dated 1875 over the town hall, and the ancient Church of St. Edmund nearby are amongst them and opposite is an old coaching inn, the Kings Arms. At the top end of the street is the old grammar school founded in 1670, a fine stone building now used as the Cookworthy Museum.

Kingsbridge Church has some interesting memorials, including a plaque by the chancel door where the body of Robert – commonly called Bone Phillip, who died on July 27th 1793 lies. At his request the tablet states:

Here I lie at the chancel door,
Here lie I because I'm poor,
The further in the more you pay
Here lie I as warm as they.

The prosperity of those early Victorian days is reflected in many splendid buildings, and today the 6,000 townsfolk enjoy one of the most pleasant and historically interesting environments to be found. The coasting vessels no longer bring general merchandise to the Quay and only private pleasure boats remind one of the sea.

Drawn by R. Worsley.

Engraved by W. Deeble.

KITLEY.

THE SEAT OF EDMUND POLLEXFEN BASTARD, ESQ.^RE

To whom this Plate is respectfully inscribed.

By 1845 the thriving woollen industry had entirely fallen away, although work was available in one of the two foundries, or with the maltsters. Like many other towns it had its fair share of small service trades and professions. It was and is a pleasant place, lively, firmly grounded in serving the prosperous agricultural area around.

At Aveton Gifford it became more interesting. Here the river Avon or Aun was seen winding through a wide vale the pasture of which had a marshy look and across the whole width of which had been thrown a bridge not much less than a quarter mile in length. To this bridge the tide reaches, flowing from the mouth of the River about four miles and bringing with it small barges, used in the conveyance of limestone. A kiln for the calcining this marble rises close upon the hither extremity of the bridge, and that it might appear ornamental from a villa a little below, hath been decorated at its angles by four turrets. I soon after reached the town of Modbury. Here I dined and about five in the evening having remounted, I passed the church with its handsome spire, seated on an eminance at its western end, and pursued the road leading to Plympton.

After two miles I came in sight of Fleet, an elegant seat of John Buttel. From the spot where I stood the whole formed a most capital landscape, and so pleasing and picturesque is it, that it cannot fail of arresting the attention, and giving delight to the most incurious traveller.

Dipping into the vale I passed the Erme by a bridge of three arches, which hath been lately erected by the County. This is known by the name of Seckers Bridge and adjoining to it near the gate that leads into Fleet, a kind of tavern hath been raised for the accommodation of the thirsty passenger.

A mile brought me to the village of Yealmpton, round which the river makes a circuit, flowing through meadows of the richest pasturage. Nothing can be more beautiful than the environs of this village. To look at them from some little distance, the whole appears a wood of Elms, the height and unpruned luxuriancy of these noble trees precluding any view of the fields which they enclose.

At a gate I soon after turned into the grounds of Kitley, seat of John Bastard Esq., one of the representatives in Parliament for the County. The house is not of modern structure, and is by no means a handsome building. It is a square, and hath a roof two thirds as high, as the front itself, being raised also with the stone of the country, a marble of a dusky hue. It stands in a most beautiful spot, enclosed as it were by two arms of the sea.

The evening now being on the wane I quitted Kitley and passing through the village of Brixton, conspicuous for its tower and the magnificent grove of elms that surround it, I soon made my approach to Plympton Earle. From the descent of a long and steep hill I had presented to me a most extensive and beautiful view. The more distant country was finely wooded and diversified with a vast number of seats, and the towns of Plympton, Ridgeway and Plympton St. Mary lay beneath me, so that I could with ease discriminate every feature that they possessed. I saw at one spot the remains of a monastry, and its richly ornamented tower, at another the relicts of an old Castle tottering with age, and nearer to me I marked the arcades of that pile which as a school house rose by the munificence of Eliza Heale about the middle of the last century.

The town of Plympton consists principally of one street of no inconsiderable length. It hath more good houses in it than almost any private town in the County and in point of situation it will yield to none.

Here I slept, and the next morning, accompanied by Mr. Jones a gentleman of the town, I rode towards Saltram, the fine seat of Lord Boringdon, the road being on the slope of a hill I had a command of the country towards the valley and of hills beyond. The church and tower of Plympton Mary were fine objects and the whole view had no less variety than beauty.

Having passed by the noble gardens we reached the Gate that leads into the park of Saltram, but as I had a desire to ride up the glen through which was the approach from Plymouth we turned right on the public road having gained a little eminence, a most enchanting scenery opened to my sight. Beneath me, the tide being up, a most beautiful lake, for so being land locked, it appeared spread itself out in a fine luminous expanse reflecting in its unruffled brown bosom, the limekilns, slate rock and houses of Crabtree on the opposite shore and on this hither side that noble stretch of woods which cloth the whole headland, and during the prime beauties of Saltram. To the right extended themselves a long line of the most verdant pastures, covered with cattle, and in the most distant point Westward appeared the town of Plymouth.

From Saltram by passing through a few of its fields I entered the road leading to the village of Plymstock, which is finely situated and attracts notice from the heights of its tower. Opposite this village I

F. W. Stockdale del.[t]

SALTRAM,

THE SEAT OF EARL MORLEY.

No. 31 of R. ACKERMANN's REPOSITORY of ARTS &c. Pub. July 1 1825.

struck down a lane to the right, wishing to see more of the estuary and soon reached a creek called Pomfleet. The scenery at this place was highly romantic.

There being no passage beneath the cliffs of Oarstone I made a short return on the road I had travelled and ascended the heights which soon brought the place to my view. The scenery was exceedingly beautiful, a complicated mixture of houses of rocks and shipping.

A long tongue of land which rose suddenly from a low flat and terminated in a conical mount like a tumulus which was a round tower, well known by the appellation of Mount Batten. At this spot nothing but the bustle and apparatus of commerce dispelled the idea of it being a lake, and of these there were abundant tokens, that assailed the ear and crowded the sight from both shores. Store houses rose on every quarter and the harbour at Catwater at this time gave commodious shelter to a vast number of merchant ships and others, who were here moored in expectation of convoy. Here also as well, and at Pomfleet, and indeed of the rocks that line the whole estuary, immense quantities of lime are burnt for the whole stratum of the county is calcareous.

Aveton Gifford is pleasantly situated in the Avon Valley, with some ancient but not outstanding houses close to the long bridge. A salmon fishery that thrived here during the first part of the eighteenth century has gone, but the beauty of the estuary, and surrounding countryside suggest that it has benefited by improvements in farming techniques.

Modbury is one of the most attractive towns in Devon, its size and quality strongly reflect the early nineteenth century, but a variety of style and colour which earlier buildings contribute heighten its attractiveness and contrast with Georgian or Victorian fronts. Like Totnes and Dartmouth it shares the vernacular slate hanging common in the South Hams. In 1850 a great cattle market was held twice a month and almost all its prosperity arose from agriculture, and this was sufficient to keep a population of 2,000.

The early years of the nineteenth century saw only a modest growth of about 200, although three nonconformist chapels were built, and the conversion of an Independent Chapel to a national school took place. Over more recent years the town, built with four main streets all downward sloping and converging at the bottom of the hills on which it is built, has doubled in size, with the consequent accretions of houses and an unhappy road widening scheme that demolished an ancient inn at the main roads junction.

Seckers Bridge is hardly noticed as a feature and Flete although still surviving was entirely remodelled in 1878 to include the original Elizabethan manor within a much grander property. The architect was Norman Shaw whose own genius is worthy of admiration, and the building is now opened to the public.

Brixton and Yealmpton have become commuting villages for Plymouth. Yealmpton has spread from the main road into the valley beneath. Fortunately most of the modern houses fit into a well tree'd landscape which helps to unify this loose-knit development and make it an attractive place in which to live, and just as good to look at.

Plympton and Plymstock are large areas of suburban development of little distinction which have since 1966 been incorporated into the administrative City of Plymouth. Until twenty years ago the ancient villages that have since been engulfed in the spread of suburbia still had clearly separate identities and characters. Most of the old villages have been preserved with some alterations within the urban spread and contain most of the attractive buildings to be found in an area which houses over 25,000 people.

A new shopping centre was built at Plymstock twenty-five years ago close to the church and inn which when seen by Swete were in the open country. Turnchapel, Hooe, Oreston, Pomphlett and Elburton were all as independent as Brixton is today. Plympton St. Mary and Plympton St. Maurice were two relatively large settlements. Plympton St. Maurice, described in such a complimentary fashion still deserves its accolade. It has kept the look of a small market town with its guildhall standing on pillars, over a pavement made with yellow Victorian paviours. The old Grammar School dating back to 1664 where Sir Joshna Reynolds went to school is used as a private school and the castle mound is now a pleasure park from which the whole of this ancient market and stannary town can be seen and enjoyed.

Plympton St. Mary which included the villages of Ridgeway, Underwood and Colebrook as well as one or two hamlets, housed about 2,750 people in 1850. Included in its boundaries was Saltram House. The groves and lawns of Saltram were already mature and a favourite spot for pinic parties. It was the largest house in the county and was enlarged during the first fifty years of the Century. Now it is owned by the National Trust, opened to the public, and probably one of the richest properties in the country.

Drawn by G. B. Campion.

Engraved by Jas. Bingley.

VIEW ON THE RIVER TEIGN,

NEAR TEIGNMOUTH DEVON.

Appendix

For students or those wishing to research in greater detail the travels and opinions of the Reverend John Swete the following volumes of his journals are available in the Devon Record Office:

Picturesque Sketches of Devon

by the Reverend John Swete

1792 – 1801

(Volumes 3, 5 and 19 were destroyed during the 1939-1945 war. Volumes 2 and 11 are war damaged and unfit for production.)

Contemporary contents list inside Volume 1

Volume 1 (1792)

Haldon House – Ashton – Canon Teign – Whiddon Park, Logan – Cromlech – Okehampton Castle – Hatherleigh – Heanton – Cross – Frithelstoke Abbey – Torrington – Bideford, Barnstaple, Ilfracombe – Comb Martyn – Linton – Castle Hill – South Molton, Tiverton, Pynes – Cowleigh, Cowick – Peamore

Volume 2 (1792)

Oxton House – Mamhead – New House – Dawlish – Teignmouth – Bishops Teignton – Whatcombe – Mary Church – Torquay, Tor Abbey – Brixham – Dartmouth – River Dart – Totnes – Austins-bridge.
(Oxton, old building p 3, new building p 7, description p 1 and 2)

Volume 3 – continuation [destroyed]

Buckfast Abbey – Dean burn – Brent – River Dart – Holne chase – Buckland – Dartmoor – Ashburton – Logan – Becky-fall – Ugbrook – Oxton – Teign River – Dunsford bridge – Clifford bridge – Great Fulford – South Zeal – Oakhampton – Waterfalls
(Oxton 170, 177, 178 no sketches of it, no views)

Volume 4 (1793) – continuation

Lidford – Cascade-bridge – Brent Tor – Lifton – Werrington – Launceston – Newbridge – River Tamar – Wear – Mt. Edgecumbe – Tavy-Wear

Volume 5 – continuation [destroyed]

Marystow – Budshead – Warleigh – Crabtree – Plympton – Ivy-bridge – Totness – Dartington – Berry Castle – Bradley – Bradley vale – Teignbridge – Ugbrook=1793. Mamhead – Parsonage – Teignmouth – Ringmore – Torr – Torquay
(Oxton five views, 134, 158, 162, 166, 165)

Volume 6 (1793) – continuation

Torquay – Torwood – Babicombe – Mill Torquay – Chapel – Torr Abbey – Ruins – Rocks – Cockington – Compton Castle – Palace Ruin Paignton – reciprocating Spring – Lupton – Dartmouth – Slapton – Salcombe – Molt – Castle Ruin

Volume 7 – continuation

Modbury – Fleet – Kitley – Saltram – Oarstone – Radford – Modbury Moreleigh – Totness – Berry Castle – Ford – Oxton – 1793 – Ashton House – Christow – Bridford – Dunsford
(Oxton mentioned p 129 no views)

Volume 8 – continuation

Clifford bridge – Rock basons – Blackistone rock – Great Fulford – Canon Teign – Crocombe bridge – Chudleigh bridge – Rock – Waterfall Episcopal Palace – Quarries Upcot – Oxton – 1804. Exminster – Topsham Retreat – Woodbury Encampment – Ottery Church – Wear on the River Otter (Oxton mentioned p 112, 113, no views)

Volume 9 – continuation

Ottery – Cadhay – Estcot – Dunkeswell Abbey – Wolford – Combe – Netherton – Colyton – Shute House – Axminster – Ford Abbey – Newnham Abbey – Ash – Lyme, Seaton, Beer

Volume 10 (1795) – continuation

Sidmouth – Otterton – Bicton – Budleigh – Exmouth – Mamhead – Oxton – 1795. Teignmouth – Shaldon, Combe, Haccombe – Ford – Bradley – Kingsteignton – Whiteway – Lindridge – Old Walls Ruins – Bitton – Dawlish
(Oxton three views of Quarry, Gateway, p 58, 62, 69)

Volume 11 (1795)
Ashcombe — Ludwell — Chapel — Brick House — Mowlish — Kenton — Kenn — Trehill — Bickham — Thornton + 1796. Netherex — Bickleigh Court — Tiverton.
(View of Oxton House page 179)

Volume 12 (1796)
Tiverton — Cove bridge — Bampton — Pixton — Dulverton — Dunster Minehead — Holnicot — Porlock — Exmoor — Linmouth — Martynhoe — Comb-Martin — Watermouth — Ilfracombe — Barnstaple

Volume 13 (1796)
Heanton Court — Tawstock — Bideford — Clovelly — Hartland Abbey — Milton Damerell — Buckland Filleigh — Heanton — Eggsford — Sandford — Creedy — Crediton — Little Fulford — Downes — Newton St. Cryres — Cowleigh — Cleve — Kenbury

Volume 14 (1796)
Totness — Cornwood — Blatchford — River Yealm — Rocks — Shaugh bridge River Plym — Swilly — Ford — Stone House — Tamerton — Crab tree — Plympton — Puslinch — Yealmpton Quarries

Volume 15 (1796)
Yealmpton Church — Wembury — Saltram — Cann Quarry — Nuneham Mills — House — Cornwood — Ashburton — Oxton. 1797 Fordland + Bridford bridge — Moreton — Fingle bridge — River Teign — Chagford — Dartmoor tin mines — Post bridge

Volume 16 and 17 (1797)
Dartmoor + Prince Hall — Dartmeet — Tavistoke — New bridge Holn bridge — Ashburton — Oxton + 1798 — River Exe — Cockwood — Cofton Chapel — Warren — Rocks — Exmouth — Powderham Castle

Volume 18 (1797)
Belvidere — Powderham Church — Nutwell — Lympstone — Quarry — Exminster — Limekilns — Countess wear — Paper Mills
(Oxton mentioned page 25, no views)

Volume 19 (1797) [destroyed]
Abbey Weir — Mt. Radford — Exeter — Bridge Castle, Cathedral, Walls

Volume 20 (1800)
Bishops Clyst — Farringdon — Grange — Cullompton — Canonsleigh — Holcomb Rogus — Bampton — Oakford bridge — Stoodley — Tiverton

The references — in brackets — to Oxton are made in pencil in the original.

Bibliography

The basis of research for each chapter has been:

Risdon, Tristram — *Survey of the County of Devon*, 1810

White's Directory, 1850

In addition:

Trevelyan, G. M. — *A Shortened History of England*

Defoe, Daniel — *A Tour through the whole Island of Great Britain*

Frazer, Robert — *General View of the County of Devon with Observations on the means of its improvements*, 1804

Newton, Robert — *Victorian Exeter*

Pevsner, Nicholas — *The Buildings of England: South Devon*; *North Devon*

Hoskins, W. G. — *Devon*; *Two Thousand Years in Exeter*

Murray's Handbook for Devon and Cornwall, 1859

Hadfield, Charles — *The Canal Age*

Cook, Olive and Smith, Edwin — *The English House through Seven Centuries*

Gloag, John — *English Furniture*

Paterson's Roads in England and Wales, 1811

Crossing's Guide to Dartmoor

A Tour in Cornwall by Rev. John Swete M.A. (Journal of the Royal Institute of Cornwall) Biographical Note by Rosemary Leach

Somers Cox, J. V. — *Devon Topographical Prints, 1660 – 1870; Catalogue and Guide*

Index

Illustrations are indicated by the heavier type